Gourmet Cooking for FREE

BRADFORD ANGIER

Illustrations by Don Berger

Willow Creek PRESS

Minocqua, Wisconsin

Please note:
Almost all of the wild game and fish mentioned in this book require
a license or a permit to hunt or trap. Seasons and restrictions vary
depending upon where you are. Some wild animals may be classified
as threatened or endangered by state or federal government, and therefore hunting them is prohibited by law. Before taking any wild game
or fish, including turtles, frogs, clams, crows, etc., check with the state
or province for wildlife hunting and fishing regulations.

For Dr. Mildred Weeks Rice,
who helped make my
Kimball Union Academy memories

Contents

7
Introduction

11
Big Game for the Gourmet
Venison • Bear • Moose • Buffalo • Caribou • Mulligan • Tongue •
Hash • Gameburgers

45
Game Birds: the Preference of Many
Grouse • Duck • Coot • Partridge • Quail • Pheasant • Goose • Pigeon • Snipe •
Woodcock • Crow • Turkey

81
Small Game: Food for a King
Beaver • Rabbit • Hare • Squirrel • Opossum • Woodchuck • Frog Legs • Porcupine •
Coon • Muskrat • Cougar

113
Fish and Its Preparation
Trout • Atlantic Salmon • Bass • Pickerel • Bullhead • Arctic Grayling • Eels

136
Shellfish You Will Enjoy
Clams • Oysters • Crabs • Crayfish • Mussels • Abalone • Scallops • Turtle

159
Edible Wild Plants: They're Everywhere
Mountain Sorrel • Scotch Lovage • Wild Celery • Wild Rice • Water Cress • Fire-weed • Nettle • Wild Onion • Wild Leeks • Mustard • Lamb's-Quarters • Dandelion • Cattail • Shepherd's-Purse • Plantain • Pursland • Wild Lettuce • Horseradish • Wild Mint • Green Amaranth • Jerusalem Artichoke • Chickweed • Sunflower • Sweet Flag • Groundnut • Irish Moss • Fiddleheads

198
Wild Fruit: Free for the Picking
Blackberries • Elderberries • Wild Strawberries • Currants • Raspberries • Wild Cranberries • Gooseberries • Blueberries • Mulberries • Run Cherries • Juniper Berries • Persimmons

220
Index of Recipes

Introduction

AMERICA GREW UP eating free foods. Today, with trout and deer even thicker in this country than during pioneer days, one out of every five Americans fishes, hunts, or does both.

As for our woodlands, marshes, fields, hillsides, pastures, and in many cases our own yards, these are luxuriant with more and more edible wild plants which now include immigrants from all over the world. Even the apartment dweller who seldom ventures beyond the ravines of the big city can often count on the generosity of his fishing, hunting and foraging friends.

In these days of soaring food prices, some of the best tasting and most healthful sustenances of all are yours for the cooking. For instance, gathering wild greens is still a happy way to sharpen a lagging appetite, even if you go no farther than to collect a bagful of common dandelions, just one of the thousands of edible wild plants in North America.

But there's more to it than that. Some of the food values of green leafy vegetables decrease as much as one-third during the first hour after picking. Even when purchased from the most modernly equipped store, they'll already have wasted away a notable share of vitamins. But gather them fresh from nature's own garden and devour them while they're at their tastiest, and you'll enjoy the finest they have to offer.

You can't buy any meat that will equal that of mountain sheep in savor. What store can supply fish as succulent as trout fresh from a mountain stream? Pheasant, woodcock, and grouse are still foremost gourmet delights. Everyone knows such pleasantly fragrant free fruits as the wild strawberry, similar to domestic species but always infinitely sweeter. Then there are the clambakes, following days enjoyed with forks and baskets on gleaming tidelands, that are flavored with all the aroma of the sea.

Nearly everybody throws back to some extent to the characteristics of his caveman ancestors and, on occasion, finds satisfaction in living for a time as a primitive man. Not the least of these atavistic instincts are the pleasures of experimenting with the free foods and the urge to be some-times independent of the market, especially when you can accomplish this in gourmet style. As La Rochefoucauld noted about the time the Pilgrims were becoming settled: To eat is a necessity, but to eat intelligently is an art.

There's this, also, as world conditions continue to worsen almost by the day. Anyone at any time could abruptly find himself dependent on his own resources for enough food to keep himself and his family alive. It costs very little in time and effort to be ready with the knowledge necessary for coping with such an emergency. If you are not ready, it could cost you your very life.

Too, when thoughtful individuals are concerned with the food supplies of present and future generations, it cer-tainly is pertinent to consider the readily available but often largely ignored wild foods. This is especially true when meals as stimulating to the palate as to the gastric juices are free for the cooking.

Chapter One

Big Game for the Gourmet

THIS COUNTRY CAME OF AGE eating venison and wearing buckskin. We were weaned as a republic on deer meat, took our first venturesome steps in deerhide moccasins, and saw our initial light through buckskin—scraped, greased, and stretched over log cabin windows in place of glass. Today, the multiplying descendants of these earlier ruminants can add much to the joys of the table.

Big game meat is like that of domestic stock, tender if it comes from young animals, when feed has been plentiful, and tough if it is from old animals. The tenderer cuts are found among muscles getting the least exercise, back muscles being more succulent than leg muscles.

Trying to judge age from antlers is not reliable. Look, instead, at the back teeth on the lower jaw. A six-month-old fawn has only four full-sized teeth on each side. A yearling, about eighteen months old during the hunting season, has five fully developed teeth to a side, with the sixth and last visible but not yet fully out of the jawbone. Then the amount of wear they show is the only indication of maturity.

The adult males, as any sportsman knows, are fattest just before the mating season which, varying according to climate and species, commences roughly in early autumn. The male becomes progressively poorer. At the end of the rut, the prime male is practically without fat, even in the normally rich marrows.

The mature female is the choice of the meat hunter once the rutting season is well under way. She remains the preference until approximately early spring. Then the male once more comes to the fore. Generally speaking, the older animals have more fat than the younger and can also be satisfactorily charmed into rare fuming steaks, pink and juicy.

The simplest way to handle big game is to have a frozen food locker plant or sometimes your butcher shop take over all the problems of skinning, aging, cutting, wrapping, labeling, and freezing in easily handled packages. In any case, the animals should first be hung in a cool, dark, dry, airy place at temperatures close to freezing for at least a week before being processed, although sometimes this is taken care of before one can get out of the wilderness.

The portions, ready to use, should be in sizes convenient for cooking all at one time. If you are doing the job yourself, wrap them snugly to eliminate air pockets in moisture-vapor-resistant coverings to make the packages airtight and thus help prevent drying. Two layers of waxed paper should be placed between any individual chops, steaks, or fillets combined in the same package so these can later be separated easily.

Freeze as quickly as possible at 0° or lower. Most frozen game can be cooked either with or without thawing. But extra cooking time must be allowed for meats not first thawed, just how much depending on the size and shape of the cut. Lower cooking temperatures are also required, or the meat will be dried on the outside before it is heated through to the center.

So you can be surer of what you are doing, you may prefer to thaw the meat first for this reason. You have to do this anyway, if a meat tenderizer is to be effective. Thawing is best accomplished, with a minimum of drying, in the refrigerator in the original wrappings.

You should use your game before the next hunting season to enjoy the best it has to offer in the way of texture and flavor. Because of its general leanness, most big game keeps particularly well. However, a fat bear should be eaten within four months to be at its best. Such delicacies as liver, heart, kidneys, and tongue will keep three months at 0°. There also are local laws governing both storage and possession limits of big game.

Grilled Venison Steaks

Grilling over open embers still is unsurpassable. However, a good ruse at the start is to get a glowing bed of coals, then to scatter on a few chips and shavings. These will flare up enough to help seal in the juices and to give that flavorsome char enjoyed by so many.

If the steak is at all fat, though, and you are using charcoal, allow this to become ash white before starting to cook. Then the drippings will not flame, and the later burning of the meat is avoided. As you are already aware, the grill should be greased beforehand to prevent sticking.

With venison in particular, where the toughening and drying effects of overcooking should be avoided if at all possible, the steaks should not be laid too near a too ardent fire. This distance should be increased, not lessened, with thicker steaks. The thicker the steak, the longer it must be cooked if the heat is to penetrate to its center. If too close too long, the exterior will overcook and toughen.

Good, tender venison will be at its sizzling best when least disguised by seasoning. All that is wanted is a scattering of salt, and maybe a melting slab of butter, just before eating.

Grill the steaks just long enough to satisfy the eater's taste. Overcooking ruins most big game meat, with the exception of bear, because of its general lack of the layers of fat common to comparable domestic cuts. Such wild meat dries out in heat, and the fibers quickly harden and toughen.

If your venison is from an older animal, treat it before cooking with a non-seasoned meat tenderizer. For the best results with game, use ¾ teaspoon per pound of meat and let it stand 20 to 30 minutes at room temperature for each ½ inch of thickness. Frozen game must, of course, be thawed first.

Pricking or gashing the steak is the most practical way to test doneness. The welling out of red juice indicates the meat is rare. If the fluid is pink, the meat is medium rare. Colorless? It's overdone, unless that's the way it is preferred.

Broiled Venison Steak

The same things said about timing and seasoning grilled venison steaks apply to these same steaks when they are broiled. Preheat the broiler. Grease the rack. Place the meat about 5 inches below the heat, depending, as already considered, on thickness. Sear quickly on both sides to conserve the juices. Then, turning as you want, cook until done to taste. Season and serve at once on hot plates.

Pan-Broiled Venison Steaks

You can achieve almost the same excellent results by pan broiling your steaks, preferably cut about 2 inches thick, in a hot bare frypan. The metal can be sprinkled with a teaspoon of salt beforehand to prevent sticking, although this is not necessary. No grease at all is used. Even that sputtering from the venison is tipped out.

Sear rapidly on both sides. Then cook with slightly less heat until done to taste. Salt and, if you wish, dust with freshly ground black pepper. Start a yellow chunk of butter melting atop each slab. Serve on hot plates.

Venison Tenderloin

Venison tenderloin, although you often can cut it with a fork, doesn't have much flavor, a failing the following recipe will pleasantly remedy. Cut your fillets 1½ inches thick. Rub liberally with rosemary. Sear them in a hot frypan with ¼ stick of butter. Then lower the heat a bit and cook for 2 minutes on each side. Season to taste with salt and freshly ground black pepper.

Add another ¼ stick of butter, 2 tablespoons brandy, and a tablespoon of Worcestershire sauce. Moving the meat and sauce about with your spatula, cook the fillets another minute on each side. Serve at once on hot plates, tipping the savory liquid over each portion of meat. When you eat these, you can almost taste the sunburned heat slanting against autumn-crowned hillsides.

Venison Steaks with Wine

Back steaks, cut from that long strip between the tops of the ribs and the spine, are always tender. But, depending on the age and the feeding habits of the animal as well as the season, they may have off flavors you'd prefer to disguise.

Cut enough steaks for two, making them 2 inches thick. Preheat a large heavy frypan over a hot fire. Brown the steaks rapidly on one side for 2 minutes. Then turn and bronze the other side for the same length of time, leaving the meat still very rare in the middle. If this does not agree with everyone's tastes, lengthen the time accordingly.

Have your wine sauce ready. This is prepared by finely chopping ½ cup of white onion and ½ cup of water cress. Move these to a bowl, stir in ½ teaspoon of ground mustard, and then add a cup of very dry sherry.

A fragrant bank of vapor will arise when this is turned over the steaks. Let everything sputter over continued high heat for 2 minutes. Then serve the steaks on their individual, heated plates with the sauce distributed over them. Hot peas and small boiled potatoes will make an adventure of this.

Venison Steaks with Pepper

Here's one that will amaze you with its deliciousness if you've never tried it before; that is, if you don't make the mistake of using ordinary ground black pepper which will be much too pungent. Instead, coarsely grind your own peppercorns in the electric blender or in a pepper mill, or crush them with a rolling pin. Even then, sift out the powdery particles for use elsewhere. You can also buy small bottles of suitable cracked or crushed peppercorns.

Cut the steaks an inch thick. Rub them with soft butter. Working one side at a time, sprinkle each slab liberally with the coarse black pepper, then press this into the meat. Let stand at room temperature for an hour.

Sprinkle a teaspoon of salt over the bottom of a very hot frypan. As soon as this begins to tan, put in the steaks. Turn once, as soon as they are well bronzed on one side. For the tenderest, tastiest meat, cook not more than 2 minutes in all.

Then knife a large chunk of butter atop each steak, sprinkle with chopped parsley and chives, set ¼ cup of warmed brandy alight with a match, pour flaming over the meat, and serve on hot plates with all the savory juices. Such steaks, robust and hearty, will make the world seem more real.

Venison Steaks and Onions

Sometimes both the flavor and texture of venison isn't all it might be—for reasons having to do with season or age—but you still want a tasty dinner for friends who perhaps are not outdoor enthusiasts.

Start the day before by trimming any fat that may have been overlooked during freezer preparation. Slice the meat about ⅝ inch thick and pound the steaks to tenderize them. For 4 or 5 pounds of meat, combine 4 teaspoons salt, 1 teaspoon freshly ground black pepper, 2 finely chopped large cloves of garlic, and rub into the meat. Sprinkle the meat with dry red wine (Burgundy or Chianti) and place in a glass or earthenware dish. Pour any remaining wine over the meat, cover the dish, and place it in the refrigerator until the decisive moment.

When the time for action arrives, heat 2 tablespoons of butter and 2 tablespoons of olive oil in a frypan until they start to darken. Then, stirring, sauté a cup of diced onion until the bits are soft and tan.

Remove them for the moment. Add more butter and olive oil in equal volumes if needed. Pat the steaks dry, sear them rapidly on both sides, then cook over slightly lower heat for 2½ minutes on each side. Return the onions and cook a minute more. With everything served sizzling hot, they'll make the flavors even more satisfying.

Venison Cutlets

Cut thin layers of otherwise tough venison across the grain from the long round leg muscle and pound them even thinner. For about a pound of these, enough for two people, beat an egg with 2 teaspoons water. Dip each cutlet in flour, then in the egg. Finally, roll in a mixture of 1½ cups fine bread crumbs, a teaspoon salt, and ¼ teaspoon freshly ground black pepper.

Allow to dry for 15 minutes. Then sauté the cutlets over low heat in a stick of butter until they are tanned short of browning. Serve with water cress and lemon wedges. This is the kind of delicately hearty meal to be particularly enjoyed when autumn is bustling out, red-faced and angry, slamming the doors of the hills behind her. Or maybe you'll prefer the following version, at least on occasion.

Venison Cutlets in Sour Cream

Cut your slices ½ inch thick from a leg of venison. For about a pound of these, enough to serve two, be melting ½ stick of butter in a large frypan. Rub salt into the cutlets with freshly ground black pepper, and then sprinkle well with flour. Brown on both sides over low heat.

Then pour a cup of sour cream over the venison. Simmer until tender. Shake on paprika and dried parsley. This is surprisingly good with hot steaming rice, mashed potatoes, buttered noodles, or spaghetti.

Roast Venison

Tender venison roasts are best cooked rare so as to take full advantage of the natural savor of the meat. If the cut isn't tender, treat it first with one of the unseasoned tenderizers.

A moderately slow oven temperature, 300° or at the most 325°, gives the best results with large roasts. Twelve minutes per pound should do it, to give you an idea. Do not follow the outdated practice of starting your roast in a very hot oven, as searing not only is unnecessary but it is inadvisable, driving out more juices than it conserves as well as toughening the game meat.

If one side of the meat is fatter, placing this uppermost on a rack in the roasting pan, with the bony side down if possible, will give you the energy-conserving advantage of some natural basting. Nevertheless, do not neglect basting, preferably with game using melted butter rather than the juices seeping from the roast. Employing a bulb-type baster rather than a gingerly wielded spoon, and after the first hour squirting all exposed parts of the roast every 15 minutes, makes this task an easy one.

Laying strips of beef fat over venison and similar big game roasts, or pinning on thick chunks of such fat, will vastly improve the final results. This practice not only deliciously adds necessary fat to the ordinarily lean venison, but it both guards the roast against high temperatures and also tends to slow down the loss of juices.

Lean, dry venison can also be improved by using a large, special larding needle and drawing thin strips of bacon or salt pork through the meat. If the flavor of your trophy is not all it might be—and the taste of different game animals of the same species varies just as much as does that of beef—you may choose to soak the fat overnight in claret flavored with garlic or a favorite seasoning, so as to introduce flavors that otherwise would permeate only a very short distance from the exterior. Venison so larded should be sliced at right angles to the strips of fat.

In any event, the roast should be taken out of the locker or refrigerator in time for its interior, as well as the outside, to warm to room temperature. The larger the cut, of course, the longer this will take.

Venison roasts should always be left uncovered, never floured, and cooked without any addition of water. Do not salt until near the finish of the cooking period or just before serving, especially as salt both draws juices from the already dry venison and does not extend its savor more than a short distance into the meat.

The insides of large roasts keep on cooking for 10 to 20 minutes after being removed from the oven, in ratio to the size of the cut and the roasting temperature. For this reason, when these portions are to be eaten cold, the overall cooking time should be abbreviated by 10 percent.

If you have a large amount of moose, deer, elk, caribou, or other game meat to eat your way through, there may be occasions when, for a special treat, you may care to modify the final flavor. There are two particularly satisfying ways in which to accomplish this. First, cut small slits in the roast and insert very thin slivers of garlic. Second, rub the meat with a damp, not wet, cloth and then with dried rosemary.

If you want gravy, deglaze the roasting pan with water or stock, stirring to remove the browned residue. Transfer this to a saucepan over low heat atop the stove. Mix a tablespoon of flour with 2 tablespoons of cold water. Add this thin paste slowly to the hot liquid, stirring constantly to avoid lumps. If necessary, a bit more flour and water stirred to a thin paste in the same proportion may be added to achieve the desired thickness. Cooking should be continued long enough to take away the raw taste of the flour.

You'll end up with a dish fit for kings and queens—or for anyone who presumed he didn't like venison.

Venison Pot Roast

For about a 4- or 5-pound chunk of one of the less tender cuts, melt ½ stick of butter in a heavy pot or saucepan whose lid fits tightly. Peel and slice 6 each of medium-size onions, carrots, and potatoes. Bronze them in the bottom of the pan. Then remove them for the moment.

Brown the meat, turning it so as to accomplish this on all sides. Then season to taste with freshly ground black pepper and with celery salt. Add a bay leaf. Pour in 2 cups of boiling stock, or 2 cups of boiling water in which 2 beef bouillon cubes have been dissolved.

Cover and place in a 350° oven for 2 hours or until a testing fork indicates that the venison is tender. Then return the vegetables and continue cooking until these, too, are done.

The dish now is ready to eat unless you expect to make a gravy. If so, remove venison and vegetables and keep in the warm oven. Taste the juice. If it needs a bit more salt and pepper, add these to taste. Then make a smooth thin paste by adding 2 tablespoons of water slowly to a tablespoon of flour, stirring constantly. When this is slowly stirred into the hot liquid, it will not form lumps in the gravy. Cook 2 minutes to take away any raw taste. Sprinkle on chopped water cress. Then serve everything, perhaps with freshly boiled noodles that have been drained and then sautéed in butter.

The resulting warmth of color, odor, and taste, spread before you on a snowy table, will combine to recall nature even in the heart of the great city.

Venison Ribs

Venison ribs, prospective titillations to the taste buds, can send such a wonderful and delightful aroma through the most aristocratic kitchen as to set your nostrils to quivering. Saw the chunks into serving pieces of perhaps 3 bones each. Salt these.

To go with about 4 pounds of ribs, enough to serve two couples, simmer for 15 minutes a cup of tarragon vinegar, 1½ tablespoons Worcestershire sauce, 1 tablespoon sugar, 1 teaspoon dry mustard, 1 teaspoon salt, and a minced garlic clove. Brush the ribs with this. Then set the pieces under a preheated broiler and cook 40 minutes, turning them every 10 minutes or brushing them again with the same sauce at the same time.

Broiled unadorned until tender, and allowed to char a bit, these ribs also are delicious without seasoning.

The ribs also can be satisfactorily baked. Place half of them in the bottom of a large roasting pan. Top with half the sauce and with sliced onion. Then cover with the second half of the ribs and roof with sliced onion and the remaining sauce. Cover and bake in a moderate 350° oven for 2 hours or until the meat loosens from the bone, removing the lid the last half hour. The resulting harmonious and subtle blend of flavors will increase your reverence for fine food.

Stuffed Venison Ribs

Moose ribs often are served this delicious way in snug homes in the big game realms of northern British Columbia. The same recipe is good with mulies and with caribou, elk, and other cousins of the deer family. Cut the ribs into serving portions. Brush with liquid smoke if you prefer. Arrange closely together in a large roaster. Start preheating your oven to a hot 450°.

For enough dressing to serve four, sauté ½ cup diced celery, ½ cup minced onion, 1 teaspoon salt, and the contents of a small can of mushroom stems and pieces in ½ stick butter for 15 minutes. Remove from the heat and stir in a cup of soft bread crumbs and 1½ teaspoons poultry seasoning.

In the meantime, brown one side of the ribs in the oven for 10 minutes. Then remove the ribs long enough to spread 2 cups of chopped, mixed carrots and celery over the bottom of the roaster. Arrange the ribs tightly together on top, their rawer sides uppermost. Cover with the dressing, smoothing it down evenly, and brown for another 10 minutes.

Then pour in either 2 cups of boiling stock or 2 cups of boiling water in which 2 beef bouillon cubes have been dissolved. Cover the roaster and return to the oven. Turn the heat down to a slow 300° and bake for 2 hours, adding more boiling water or stock if necessary. This is food you'll remember afterwards with a fond sigh.

"Boiled" Game

You'll often find this becomes your favorite way of cooking when you have a few hundred pounds of deer, moose, caribou, elk, antelope, buffalo, and the like to eat your way through. However, the word "boiled" should be a misnomer. This game will be better if cooked at temperatures no higher than a simmer.

Simmering does not mean boiling gently. Boiling is boiling, and it robs the dryish game meat in particular of flavor and tenderness. Simmering is some 25° cooler, and it can make all the difference. If you do not cook by thermometer, which for simmering should be in the vicinity of 185° at sea level instead of at boiling's 212° at the same elevation, watch for the first bubbles. As soon as any appear, either immediately lower the heat or move the receptacle to another burner or to a cooler part of the stove or fire.

Place about a 4-pound chunk of game in a heavy iron skillet, large kettle, or small Dutch oven in which it fits with reasonable snugness. Cover with bubbling water. Bring to a simmer. After a few minutes, skim.

Then add salt and freshly ground black pepper to taste, 2 level teaspoons of the former being about right. Also put in half a dozen small peeled onions, a small chopped stalk of celery with the leaves, ½ teaspoon thyme, and a bay leaf. Simmer about an hour for each pound of meat, at the end of which time the game should be tender but not stringy or mushy.

This is absolutely superb hot. Any you plan to eat cold should be allowed to cool in the broth. Then move it to a flat utensil that also will hold a bit of the liquid. Press the portion into shape with a weighted plate so it can later be more handily sliced. Such creations, all the more wonderful for being simple, will be a monument to your skill and judgment as an epicure.

Venison Dumplings

One utterly delicious way to use the remaining broth is with meat dumplings. For these latter, grind a pound of venison with ½ pound of beef fat. Mix with a cup of bread crumbs moistened with a bit of the broth, ¼ cup grated onion, a teaspoon salt, and ¼ teaspoon freshly ground black pepper.

If you serve these dumplings frequently, vary the taste on occasion by adding ⅛ teaspoon cinnamon, ⅛ teaspoon allspice, and a tablespoon of fresh lemon juice.

Bind everything together with 3 beaten egg yolks. Mold into small balls. Roll in flour and simmer 30 minutes, tightly covered, in enough broth to go around.

Venison Meat Loaf

The preceding meat mixture—especially when prepared with the cinnamon, allspice, and lemon juice—is so grand a way to use the tougher cuts of venison that on occasion, when you want to let the cooking more or less take care of itself, you may want to turn it into a meat loaf.

Just pack the mixed ingredients in a well-buttered casserole. Cover with a can of tomato or mushroom soup, if you are in a hurry, and bake in a moderate 350° oven for an hour.

If you've a little extra time, however, this meat loaf is worth the effort of an onion cream sauce in place of the prepared soup. Simmer a diced, medium-size yellow onion 5 minutes with ¼ cup of water. Then, draining off any excess liquid, sauté until soft but not brown in 2 tablespoons of butter. Add a cup of light cream, cover, and cook another 5 minutes over low heat, stirring occasionally. Cascade this over the venison loaf and bake as before.

Mulligan

Personal tastes and ingenuity, as well as available ingredients, have over the centuries usually dictated the mulligans along the dwindling American frontiers. However, the following well-proved recipe is a good basis from which to proceed in the city kitchen, especially when twilight is in the blues of the foothills and rolling like fog up the streets, catching in the branches of the scattered trees.

Cut about 2 pounds of venison into 1-inch cubes. Roll the meat lightly in flour seasoned with salt and freshly ground black pepper. Sauté a cup of chopped onion until limp in the bottom of a heavy kettle. Then brown the meat. If you favor what garlic can do for a stew, add a clove of this herb, minced.

Pour in 4 cups of water, cover, and simmer until the meat

is nearly tender. Add a cup of peas, 4 small diced potatoes, 4 small diced carrots, and 2 tablespoons chopped parsley. Cook until everything is tender.

You can, then, thicken the broth with a thin flour and water paste if you wish, correct the seasoning with pepper and salt if necessary, and serve.

Such a mulligan, thickened or not as you prefer, is also excellent with the traditional dumplings. A good way to go about these tasty and quickly done tidbits is by sifting together 2 cups of flour, 1 tablespoon baking powder, and 1 teaspoon salt. Work in a tablespoon of butter. When everything is ready to go, pour ¾ cup of milk into a cavity dented in the center of the flour mixture. Mix everything together very lightly and rapidly, using a folding motion.

Have the mulligan bubbling gently, not rapidly, as this would break up the dumplings. Immediately place a single layer of rounded tablespoonfuls of the batter in the broth atop the solids. Cover at once and allow the dumplings to steam for 15 to 20 minutes, whereupon the dumplings should be light and feathery. To keep them this way, serve them to one side of the gravy. Mulligans such as this will tantalize your nostrils and make your salivary glands work overtime, especially when snow is falling outside and the wind is driving it against the windows.

Gameburgers

Ground venison, properly prepared, has fewer wild flavors than steaks or roasts. The main essential is to include as much beef fat as you like to lighten your ground beef.

Also, if this should be necessary, trim the meat well, removing any deer fat or any dried or discolored portions before consigning it to the grinder. Otherwise, gameburgers can include venison that is below par in tenderness and plumpness.

Seasonings go better if mixed directly with the venison when the meat is to be used at once, *not* however if it is scheduled for freezing. For each pound of gameburger, ½ teaspoon of salt and ⅛ teaspoon of freshly ground black pepper is ordinarily sufficient. You may also like to include ¼ teaspoon of mustard. Shredded cheddar cheese, about ½ cup to each pound of meat, also blends well.

Gameburgers are best when they accumulate the charred, smoky taste associated with grilling. They are next best pan broiled with just enough butter to prevent sticking. If you like them rare, that's all to the good. They toughen rapidly when cooked too long. Serve the way you like, perhaps with salted slices of tomato and wisps of lettuce, and have plenty for replacements.

Marrow

The mineral-rich marrow found in big game bones is not surpassed by any other natural food in nourishment. What is, at the same time, the most delectable of tidbits, is wasted by overcooking. Just saw the large marrowbones into convenient lengths, perhaps 4 to 6 inches long. Simmer no more than 10 minutes, or roast in a moderate 350° oven for ½ hour or until the prongs of a carving fork penetrate easily into these soft vascular tissues.

Unless you have marrow forks or scoops, push out the hot marrow with thin knives or with slim wooden sticks, whittled flat at one end. We enjoy this exceedingly tasty marrow as is, although you can salt and pepper it if you wish and supplement it with crisp toast.

Broiled Big Game Liver

Big game liver is so highly pleasing that it's too bad that more do not have the opportunity of feasting on it. However, it is usually enjoyed in camp while the body of the meat is taking on flavor and tenderness. If you get it out of the woods in time, you can satisfactorily fast-freeze it and keep it up to three months at 0° in the freezer. Only that of the polar bear, and incidentally of the ringed and bearded seal, is inedible because of a seasonal overabundance of Vitamin A. It's difficult to distinguish any difference in taste between venison and other big game liver and the choicest butcher shop delicacy.

Slice about ¾-inch thick. Brush with melted butter. Broil on a greased rack, with the top of the meat 2 inches from the heat, about 2 minutes a side until well browned outside and still red and juicy within. There will be those who'll prefer their liver done somewhat more than this. Overcooking, however, gives you a leathery, tasteless, and far less nutritious dish.

As soon as the liver is ready, salt and pepper it to taste. Fresh game liver also is delectable without any seasoning at all, quite a few hunters broiling it this way beside open fires immediately after they have downed their trophies. When you eat liver like any of this, you can almost savor the pine woods.

Liver and Bacon

Liver and bacon are traditional. Start the bacon first in a cold pan. Sauté slowly, moving and turning the pieces from time to time. If you like your bacon crisp, keep pouring off the grease. You'll want only a small amount for the liver.

In the meantime, prepare some onions. These may be either chopped or thinly sliced. When the bacon is done, cook the onions slowly in the fat until golden and tender. Then remove from the pan, season with salt, and keep warm along with the bacon until the liver is ready. While this latter is briefly sautéing, about a minute to a side, be draining the bacon on absorbent paper. Everything will then be a delight to the taste buds.

Simmered Heart

Cut the heart into ½-inch cubes. Roll in flour that has been seasoned with 1 teaspoon salt and ¼ teaspoon freshly ground black pepper. Brown lightly in butter. Then add 2 cups boiling water and simmer 30 minutes.

Or, if you'd like a real feast, place about a pound of cubed heart into enough cold water, along with ½ teaspoon salt, so you'll end up with 2 cups of broth. Simmer until the bits of heart are tender.

Now get 2 tablespoons butter melting in a frypan. Sauté ½ cup diced onion and ½ cup chopped celery in this over low heat until tender. Gradually add 2 tablespoons flour, stirring until it is smooth and thick. Then slowly stir in the 2 cups of broth and continue to cook over low heat, stirring constantly, until the gravy is smooth and thickened.

The heart goes in next. Stir everything together over low heat. If you want the gravy a little thinner or a bit whiter, add either cream or evaporated milk. Salt and pepper to taste. Top with paprika and parsley flakes and serve while steaming. I will personally certify that you have never before tasted heart like this.

Broiled Kidneys

Delicate big game kidneys are like hearts and livers in that the slightest overcooking will both toughen them and rob them of flavor. Incidentally, despite the instructions set forth in numerous recipes, there is no need to soak kidneys or any other part of game beforehand. Try soaking a prime steak sometime.

Kidneys are divided according to size. Those from small deer and caribou often are halved or quartered lengthwise. Those from moose and elk may be sliced. The only thing you have to do with perhaps the best of the lot, bear kidneys, is to pull away the connective tissue.

Broiled kidneys are taste-tempting if not overdone. Heat quickly for 3 minutes on one side, then for 2 minutes on the other side, or to your personal taste. Baste several times with good, honest butter. When they are done, season them with salt and freshly ground black pepper. Try serving with fresh water cress. They'll have an air of luxury to them.

Sautéed Kidneys

Butter is excellent for sautéing thinly sliced big game kidneys, bacon and sausage being too strong for most palates. Get the butter warm first, over heat not ardent enough to brown it. Fork the kidneys around during some 4 minutes they are cooking, salting and peppering them to taste. Then remove to a warm place.

Stir a tablespoon of diced mild onion into the juices. Cook until soft but not golden. Add 4 tablespoons of good, dry sherry and cook this until everything thickens. Strew lightly with cayenne pepper. Then pour everything over the kidneys and serve. This can be a tantalizing feast indeed.

Kidneys Flambé

This can become an esteemed dish, particularly during crisp hunting weather. Cut or divide two deer kidneys or their equivalent into segments about the size of acorns. Brown 3 minutes in hot butter. Then add 2 jiggers of warmed brandy and set alight.

When the blue flames die, add ⅓ cup good, dry sherry, ½ cup sliced fresh mushrooms, and a tablespoon chopped onions. Bring to a simmer. In about 10 minutes or as soon as the mushrooms are tender, add ½ cup heavy cream, a tablespoon lemon juice, and a teaspoon of prepared horseradish. Season to taste with salt and freshly ground black pepper. Stirring, bring rapidly to a simmer. Serve at once on crisp toast or on hot crusty biscuits, streaming with butter. I don't know of a tastier way of ushering in the hunting season.

Big Game Tongue

Tongue, on the other hand, needs at least 4 or 5 hours of cooking, although it, too, should never be soaked beforehand. Settle for scrubbing it well. Then cover with boiling water. Add several onions, a peeled clove of garlic, ½ teaspoon basil, a bay leaf, and a liberal amount of salt.

Simmer until you can easily insert and withdraw a sharp fork. Allow to cool in the same liquid until it can be handled easily enough to skin and bone. The tongue then can be reheated in its own juice before serving, thinly sliced, or it can be enjoyed cold.

Or, if you have something as large as a moose tongue, you may care to transfer the tender and peeled tongue to a baking dish. Mix a small can of tomatoes, a sliced onion, a cup of tarragon vinegar, ½ stick melted butter, a teaspoon smoked salt, ½ teaspoon nutmeg, ¼ teaspoon cinnamon, and ⅛ teaspoon cloves. Pour over the tongue and bake in a slow 300° oven for 2 ½ hours. Serve with hot mashed potatoes or hot biscuits, either well enriched with butter. Somehow, this repast carries with it some of the charm of bygone days when such delicacies were more universally esteemed.

Big Game Hash

For a really splendiferous taste, especially if you help matters along with the distinctive flavors of wild greens, start by dicing 2 large onions, then sautéing them in ½ stick of butter until they are soft but not brown.

Then tan 2 cups of diced, freshly boiled potatoes with the onions and butter. Add ½ cup of cooked, well drained, cut-up greens such as dandelions or mustard and stir that around a bit. Two cups of diced, cooked game meat go in next.

Moisten all this with ½ cup of stock from the meat or vegetables, seasoned with a crushed garlic clove, a teaspoon of salt, ⅛ teaspoon freshly ground black pepper, ½ teaspoon ginger, and ¼ teaspoon of monosodium glutamate.

Arrange in a pan in the shape of an omelet. Bake in a moderate 350° oven for 15 minutes. Then scatter some chips of butter on top and finish by browning under the broiler. You can almost hear the creaking wheels of covered wagon trains when you eat grub like this.

Bear

You'll probably have to try it to believe it, but properly cooked bear meat is comparable to the best prime beef. However, bear steaks are never satisfactory. The meat is essentially stringy, and because of a possibility of trichinosis it must be cooked too long to make a good steak. Unlike other game meats, bear should always be well done. The generally inherent fat will prevent it from drying out, as the extra heat makes it all the more savory.

Roast Bear

Except in the spring, trim off all but about ½ inch of fat. In the springtime, when the bear generally is lean from hibernation, lard liberally with beef fat. Too, when the bear is lean, baste all exposed portions about every 10 minutes after the first hour. Handiest for this? One of those bulb-type basting devices that resemble an oversize eye dropper.

Place the meat, with the bone if any toward the bottom, on a rack in an open pan. Don't flour or sear. Moderately slow heat, about 325°, will give the best results. Bear varies considerably in texture, so the only rule that can be given is to roast it until tender. When a large sharp fork can be easily inserted, then withdrawn without binding, the meat will be ready.

Because of the absolutely delightful aroma given off by roasting bear, so will everyone else.

Bear Stew

Trim off most of the fat. Cut the meat into small pieces, such as 2-inch cubes, keeping the size and shape of these uniform so the cooking will be even. Most of the year you can brown bear meat in its own fat in the bottom of the pan. The rest of the time, start with a small amount of beef fat or with butter. For about a 4-pound chunk, sauté a large sliced onion at the same time.

Add enough boiling water to cover the meat. Cover tightly and simmer, not boil, until a tested chunk of meat proves to be barely tender. Then add 4 quartered medium-size potatoes, 4 small sliced carrots, 2 small sliced parsnips, a cup of diced celery, and a dozen small white onions. Cook a few more minutes until everything is tender, salt and pepper to taste, and serve.

Incidentally, it's a good idea to make more of this bear stew than you can use at one sitting, as even its originally savory flavor improves each time it is reheated.

Bear Chops

Trim all but about ¼ inch of any fat from the ribs. Rub them well with salt and about ¼ as much freshly ground black pepper. Set in one layer in a pan, nearly cover with water, bring to a simmer, and cook 15 minutes.

Now spread 2 tablespoons of raw, quick-cooking brown rice on each chop. Then in order put on each chop a slice of tomato, a slice of onion, and a slice of green pepper. Top with fresh mushrooms that are still warm from being sautéed in butter. Sprinkle with paprika. Add enough boiling water to reach the level of the rice. Cover and cook ½ hour or until the chops with their full and flavorsome deliciousness are well done.

Bear Cracklings

You'll be passing up some of the best shortening available anywhere if you don't render all bear fat in moderate heat in open oven pans, then strain the liquid into jars. That from the black bear will harden into a clear white lard, while that from the grizzly will remain a more easily measured oil. The remaining cracklings are tasty and pleasingly crisp to nibble at.

You might also like to liven a dinner with some sturdy and forthright crackling bread, so popular during pioneer years. Just sift together 2 cups yellow corn meal, a teaspoon baking soda, and a teaspoon salt. Combine 2 slightly beaten eggs with a cup of buttermilk or sour milk. Stir this into the

corn meal mixture, along with ¾ cup fine crushed bear cracklings.

Form into individual cakes, place on a well buttered pan,
and bake in a preheated hot 400° oven about ½ hour or until
an inserted toothpick comes out dry.

Moose Nose

"The great delicacies of the North American wilderness,"
Vilhjalmur Stefansson, most eminent of the recent explorers,
told me a few years ago, "are moose nose, beaver tail, buffalo
hump, caribou brisket, and ling liver, all of them the delicious
fat that it is now the fashion to condemn."

Like Dr. Stefansson, I've also enjoyed all these. Especially
when open flames are flickering in fireplace or barbecue pit,
and there's the added relish of good companionship, it would
be hard to pick five free edibles that are more delicious.

Moose nose is a favorite among Indians and many sour-
doughs in the northwestern wilds of the continent where I've
enjoyed log-cabin living during much of the past three
decades. It's just as heartwarming in the city. The way you go
at it with this biggest of all deer, prehistoric or otherwise, is
to cut off the large upper jaw just below the eyes.

Don't try to skin this. Instead, scald it in a pot of bubbling
water, simmer about an hour, cool, and pluck. Then cook just
short of boiling in fresh water, along with salt and pepper
and, if you like, onions, until the white meat falls away from
the nostrils and dark strips loosen from the bones and jowls.

In the meantime, the kitchen will be sending out tantalizing clouds of pure wilderness splendor, presaging a warm, sweet, odorous feast.

This is fine to pick at hot. If you can keep occupied with other tidbits, though, let the juices and the meat jell together, then savor the whole in cold slices.

Buffalo Hump

With buffalo now legal game around Canada's Great Slave Lake and occasionally in our forty-ninth state, and with surplus bison regularly being harvested elsewhere in both countries, buffalo hump is again being savored by more and more Americans and Canadians.

When I can come by a substantial chunk, with its characteristic streaks of orange fat, I like to salt it lightly, then shove it into a moderately warm 350° oven, with the fattest portion uppermost, to roast slowly, uncovered, while basting itself to a turn. This is much too good, a lot of us figure, to serve any other way but rare.

Caribou

Caribou, North America's most abundant big game animal, is unforgettable, particularly when you're able to choose mature animals in their prime. Clouds and cold September rain closed down on me one time in the northern British Columbia mountains after we'd dropped a fat trophy bull when it was at its sleekest and tastiest just before the rut. The mist was too thick for hunting, which made the fire in the cook tent all the cozier. Incidentally, I still cook caribou the same way even when surrounded by the most modern of culinary conveniences.

Having plenty of leisure this particular day, we got things going by sautéing a cup each of chopped onion and chopped celery in 2 tablespoons of honest butter, along with the contents of a small can of mushrooms. This we seasoned with a teaspoon of salt, then mixed a cup of dry bread crumbs with it.

We spooned the lot over 4 thick slices of caribou brisket—enough, we reckoned, for two hungry men. These went into a flat pan and a hot 425° oven. After the meat had browned for 10 minutes, we turned it to bronze for 10 minutes on the other side. By this time, the hardwood in the sheet-metal stove had fallen into coals which, with occasional replenishments, maintained a low, even heat for the next hour. We couldn't have waited any longer, anyway.

While we were eating, the nearby horse bells seemed to become louder and more distinct. When we shoved the whipping canvas flaps aside, it was to find a breeze scudding through the peaks and the air nearly clear. We glassed a couple of heavy-headed shapes on the cliffs opposite. Two days later we were broiling savory Stone-sheep steaks, one delicacy omitted by Dr. Stefansson that I'd surely include among this continent's treats.

Mountain Sheep

This most coveted prize among North America's big game animals furnishes the best eating you're ever likely to find on this earth. The superlative meat is cooked like venison, although many don't want anything impinging upon the ambrosial natural flavor but salt, butter, and perhaps a little freshly ground black pepper. When you're making stews, it's advisable to stick to the blander vegetables such as carrots, potatoes, and parsnips for this reason.

Wild mint (*Alentha*), though, is pleasing with large rare roasts. You can make a sauce of this by heating ½ cup mild vinegar, ⅓ cup sugar, and ¼ teaspoon salt. Stir in finely chopped young mint leaves to taste, about ⅓ cup, and let the sauce cool an hour before serving. But even this wild mint sauce, you'll find, should be used sparingly with this king of the epicurean repasts.

Chapter Two

Game Birds:
The Preference of Many

FOR NOTEWORTHY DINING there's nothing like the game birds that carry with them the savor of smoky upland afternoons and of windy mornings relished in companionable blinds.

There isn't, that is, if one takes into account that wild fowl, having to forage more energetically for scanter fare, are considerably leaner than domestic poultry. Flavorsome substitutes must be provided for this missing fat. Even more important, every care must be taken to avoid the overcooking that will result in a tough, dry, stringy, thoroughly tasteless bird.

As for washing or soaking in water, whether salted or fresh, this has never helped the flavor of any game. All that will be called for, at most, will be wiping with paper toweling or with a clean damp cloth.

The age of the game bird is an important consideration. With young geese and ducks, the tips of the outermost tail feathers end in a V-shaped notch. By autumn, these feathers will have been nearly all moulted or lost and replaced by plumage with rounded or pointed tips. Therefore, if the fowl you shoot has even a solitary V-tipped tail feather, it's a youngling. If all tips are pointed or rounded, it's probably an oldster, although especially late in the season the possibility remains that it is a fully moulted young bird.

If you are lucky enough to collect a wild turkey, there's a foolproof tenderness test. As soon as you come up to your trophy, fan the tail feathers. If the tips are all even, it's an older bird. But if the pair of central feathers obviously protrudes beyond the rest, you have a bird-of-the-year and peak eating.

Two basic tests will give you an accurate answer with pheasants. First, look at the leg spurs. With old ringnecks, they're dark, glossy, sharply pointed, and many times slightly curved like a thorn. With youngsters, they're light colored, dull, relatively stubby, and often cone-shaped. If you still have doubts, hold the fowl by its lower bill, with your thumb in its mouth, and give it a little shake. If the lower jaw breaks, odds are it's a young bird, fit to broil or fry.

Longevity doesn't make so much difference when you're cooking the small game birds. But, for the record, the best clues offered by quail, grouse, and Hungarian partridge are the major wing feathers. In young birds, the tips of the outermost two on each wing are more pointed than the rest.

One axiom, which pretty well holds for all upland game birds, is particularly handy if you've plucked your trophies before remembering to check their age. In old birds, the tip of the breastbone is rigid. In most younglings, you can easily bend the tip with one finger.

Game birds, being generally lean, are particularly adapted for keeping in the freezer. However, federal regulations make it illegal to possess migratory waterfowl for more than ninety days after the close of the regular season. They further provide that feet, head, and head plumage must remain intact. There are also some state laws governing the storage of game birds that may need individual checking.

Before freezing, the fowl should be prepared according to the way you plan to cook it. When the bird is left whole, giblets and neck can be wrapped in freezer paper and left inside the cavity. Too, such parts from a number of birds can be collected in a single package and kept for up to three months before you enjoy that soup. Otherwise, package, freeze, store, and eventually thaw game birds according to the suggestions already made for the handling of big game.

Spitted Grouse

On this young continent even city dwellers live close to their wilderness background, and the campfire continues to be part of America's pioneer heritage, although today it often finds expression in the rotisserie. Seldom are these instincts aroused any more strongly than when we're rotating a sputtering brace of grouse.

An hour before cooking, rub the pair of birds inside and out with 8 parts of salt and 1 of freshly ground black pepper. When ready to go, brown a medium-size chopped onion with a stick of butter in a pan. Add ½ teaspoon tarragon, ⅛ teaspoon thyme, a tablespoon lemon juice, and either a cup of dry white wine, or a cup of hard cider plus a jigger of apple-jack. Cover and simmer 10 minutes.

Spit the grouse, brush liberally with the sauce, and dust with parsley flakes and paprika. Place the drip pan in position. Frequently brushing the birds with the basting sauce and then with the taste-tingling drippings, turn them until they are so golden and tender that a famished man can't wait any longer.

Roast Grouse

Grouse is so delicately flavored that it is unfortunate when it is served with strong-tasting foods. A big dish of water cress, shoestring potatoes, and toast well covered with the giblets that have been chopped and then sautéed in butter are about right.

By the same criterion, you'll do well to elect to bypass the often elaborate dressings suggested for this game bird. At the most, stuff with sliced apple and diced celery. Rub well with butter. Place breast side up in a shallow roasting pan and bard with thin slices of salt pork.

Roast grouse is best rare. Allow about 30 to 40 minutes, or until done, in a slow 300° oven, brushing often with melted butter. For an occasional taste change, if you ever want one, blend a good sauterne or, if you prefer, fresh lemon juice with the butter.

When a sharp fork can be easily inserted and withdrawn, remove the salt pork from the grouse. Brush again with the melted butter. Then turn the heat up to a very hot 500° just long enough to give the fowl an appetizing tan. Try this suggestion when snow, falling ceaselessly and without sound outside the dining room, seems to be imposing a perpetual silence on everyone, broken only by the satisfied clink of silverware.

Broiled Grouse

The grouse, as distinctive in the field as on the table, has such a naturally delicate flavor and texture that it needs no fancy accompaniments.

Just split the birds. Rub them well with butter, salt, and a little freshly ground black pepper. Broil them either over glowing coals or in a broiler for about a dozen minutes, turning them several times during the process. The same accompaniments as for roast grouse will be fine. This will really recall the heartwarming afternoons and nights of autumn.

Creamed Grouse

When grouse are plentiful, that's the time to dine sumptuously on the delicate meat of the legs and breast, creamed. The giblets and the rest can later be transformed into an elegant soup.

Dredge legs and breasts with flour that has been seasoned with salt and freshly ground black pepper. Now bring 6 slices of bacon, more if necessary, slowly to a sputter in a heavy frypan, starting with the pan cold. When the bacon is crisp, remove it to a hot platter. Quickly brown the grouse on both sides in the fat. Then lower the heat, cover, and cook 15 minutes, turning at about the halfway point.

Put the grouse on the hot platter with the bacon. Stir 2 tablespoons of flour into the fat and juices. Still stirring, add 1 ½ cups of light cream. When this has thickened, check the seasoning. Let each banqueter spoon his share over grouse, bacon, and any vegetables. This is food you're never going to forget.

Roast Wild Duck

Wipe the duck with a damp cloth but, as with all game, do not wash. Rub inside and out with a teaspoon of salt and ⅛ teaspoon of freshly ground black pepper. To help along the flavor, put a few apple slices, several small peeled onions, some chopped celery, a sprig of parsley, and a half dozen juniper berries inside each canvasback, mallard, black duck, or such. This filling is discarded after roasting. Skewer the opening.

Rub the bird liberally with soft butter. Place on a rack in a small pan. Heat the oven before setting in the bird, its breast pinned with 5 or 6 strips of salt pork. Pour a blend of ¼ cup claret and ¼ cup of water over it.

Roast at a hot 450° for 20 minutes; a correspondingly shorter time if your duck is a pintail, teal, or one of the other smaller varieties. You'll find that with the meat looking almost raw this way, you'll be able to enjoy duck night after night during the gunning season. Basting every 5 minutes, and at the same time brushing with melted butter, will do much to improve the flavor. It will certainly sharpen the appetite.

There is argument about the heat at which duck can be most advantageously roasted. Perhaps you can settle this to your own liking. Try one sometime in a moderate 325° oven for about 45 minutes.

Roasting an Old Duck

A lot of hunters like their wild ducks best roasted. You can still satisfy this preference when the bird is old and tough. Part of the secret? First simmer it slowly in salted water, with a handful of celery leaves added, until tender.

This removes so much of the flavor that some find objectionable that you may then care to stuff the fowl. If so, for each bird sauté ½ cup of diced onion in 2 tablespoons of butter until soft but not brown. Mix this with some cooked brown or wild rice well seasoned with salt and freshly ground black pepper, an equal bulk of diced raw apple, and a scattering of seedless raisins that have been soaked in a little water for ½ hour. Sew or skewer this dressing in place.

Rub the duck well with paprika and salt, crisscross liberally with bacon, pour a cup of good red wine over everything, and roast in a moderate 325° oven until browned, basting frequently. It will then be ready to fall apart at the touch of a fork.

Ducks Roasted in Foil

For strips of steaming duck meat that will warm a hungry man's heart, you may want to wait until the end of the season so you may select the plumpest, primest birds available. Since you can plan on ½ to 1 cup of stuffing per pound of dressed fowl, the following stuffing will be sufficient for two average mallards or canvasbacks, three pintail, four wood ducks, or five to six teal.

Place gizzards and hearts, cut into small cubes, in a small saucepan. Pour over them the liquid from a can of mushroom stems and pieces, and simmer gently for 15 minutes. Meanwhile, melt 2 tablespoons of butter and sauté the diced duck livers for 2 to 3 minutes. Combine the diced giblets, the butter and mushroom liquid along with the reserved mushroom pieces. Season with 1 teaspoon salt, ¼ teaspoon pepper, ½ teaspoon thyme. Pour over 3 cups of crumbled day-old white bread and toss lightly with a fork to blend. The stuffing will appear rather dry, but the delectable juices produced by cooking the ducks in foil will moisten it to the proper extent.

Rub each duck liberally inside and out with butter, sprinkle with salt and a little ginger. Stuff the cavities lightly with the dressing, so that it will have room to expand during the cooking. Lay each duck on a large doubled rectangle of heavy-duty aluminum foil and wrap, crimping all edges tightly. Arrange on a shallow pan and ease into a preheated hot 400° oven. After 10 minutes, when the birds have begun to sputter, reduce the heat to a moderate 325° for 2 hours for the larger ducks, a correspondingly shorter time for the wood ducks or teal.

If you restrain yourself from unwrapping these fowl to brown them, you will be rewarded with moist birds swimming in juices. Serve a cupful of this with each portion so the diner can dip each forkful of steaming bird into its gratifying flavor. A water cress salad, dressed with wine vinegar and freshly ground black pepper and just a little oil, goes well with this duck, especially if a north wind is blowing gusts of snow against the windows like charges of chilled shot.

Braised Wild Duck

When the feet and beaks of your ducks are horny, marks of advanced years, it is not a bad idea to begin thinking of braising. Stuff each fowl with apples, celery, and onion, sliced in equal amounts. Place in a roaster, along with a sliced onion and 4 stalks of celery that are complete with leaves. Pour in ½ inch of boiling water.

Cover and cook in a slow 325° oven for an hour, adding any boiling water that may be needed to maintain the ½-inch level. Then uncover, lightly encrust the duck with a grating of orange rind, and cook with the lid off 30 minutes longer.

Remove the stuffing, sprinkle each duck with a tablespoon of fresh orange juice, place on a heated platter and keep hot while you prepare the sauce. Strain the pan juices into a saucepan and boil rapidly until the liquid is reduced to 2 cups. Check the seasoning, adding a jigger of brandy if you wish, and remove from the heat.

Thicken with beurre manié, made by kneading 2 tablespoons of butter with 3 tablespoons of flour until a smooth paste is achieved. With a wire whip, beat the beurre manie into the hot liquid, then return to a low flame. Stirring constantly, bring the sauce to a simmer and continue to stir at a simmer for a minute or two, until the sauce is thick enough to coat a spoon.

Wild rice and highbush cranberry jelly make a savory accompaniment, especially when the full moon is shining into the room, laying a pattern of the windows on the carpet.

Broiled Wild Duck

Split the ducks along their backs. Rub with salt and freshly ground black pepper in the proportion of 4 to 1 respectively. Then brush liberally with melted butter. Broil until tender, brushing frequently with either melted butter or with an equal volume of melted butter and good port. This is something to enjoy on the terrace as day shades into night.

Breast of Wild Duck Sautéed

When bags have been full, you may enjoy the particular pleasure of sitting down to a feast of just duck breasts, saving the remainders of the birds for soups or fricassees. Heat butter or a blend of butter and olive oil in a large skillet over moderately high heat. Meanwhile, pat the duck breasts dry with paper towels so they will brown quickly and not steam. When the butter foam subsides, the fat is hot enough. Sauté the duck portions briefly so they will be browned on the outside, yet still slightly rare. Then season with salt and freshly ground pepper.

Roast Coot

It has been said that individuals raised on the seaboard have a natural palate for coot, whereas an inlander is apt to find them too fishy. A good way around, in any event, is to rub a brace of the skinned birds, which can be used the same day they are shot, liberally with a stick of butter mixed with ½ cup of bacon drippings, both allowed to stand at room temperature until soft.

Cut an apple and an onion in two, and place ½ of each in each bird. Roast in a hot 425° oven for 15 minutes or until tender, frequently brushing with the drippings. Then remove the apple and onion.

For the gravy, add ½ cup heavy cream and ½ cup of fine red Burgundy to the drippings and scrapings in the pan, quickly stirring to a simmer atop the stove. Cascade over the coot, now steaming atop a nest of wild rice on a hot platter, and serve. You can almost taste the fine sensuous delight of sparkling surf, the water-drenched rocks, and the vigor of the gulls screaming in the fine, free air, when you sit down to coot like this.

Northern Partridge

The most memorable roast partridge I ever ate goes back to a day when I was alone in a small log cabin in the Far North, with the temperature hovering a frigid 50° below zero. The two birds were big and old, but I had all day with nothing to do but keep a wood fire stoked up and to sit close beside it with a Dumas book, while outside trees and river ice snapped and banged as they froze even more deeply.

I wanted a moist stuffing, from ingredients at hand, so I mixed well-soaked dried apples in equal amounts with cream cheese, and stirred in a minced clove of garlic and 4 table-spoons of rendered bear fat. Butter, I proved later, would have served almost as well.

The brace of partridge, well rubbed with the fat and criss-crossed with bacon, went into a bread pan apiece and into the hot oven. There I basted them with their own juices about every half-hour until the meat was falling away from the bones, by which time it was deliciously permeated with the savor of the dressing.

Roast Partridge

All you have to do is rub each drawn and cleaned bird inside and out with salt and butter, bard well with thin slices of salt pork, and roast in a slow 300° oven for 30 to 40 minutes or until tender, periodically brushing with melted butter. Remove the salt pork for the last 10 minutes. When the partridge are bronzed and beckoning, see if you don't like sprinkling them generously with bread crumbs that have been browned in butter.

The partridge is a dry bird, so you may appreciate a gravy. To flavor it, use the drippings and all the brown coating you can scrape off the roaster. Stir 2 tablespoons of flour into this. Add the chopped giblets and 2 cups of the stock in which these have been simmered until tender. Season to taste with salt and freshly ground black pepper. Stir and simmer until thick. This brings back crisply hot autumn afternoons when shade and light shred the coloring of the uplands between them.

Partridge in Mustard Leaves

Partridge are frequently so plentiful that, on occasion, you may like to try something different with them. Allowing one fowl per diner, rub well with fresh lemon juice. Then, depending on how many birds you're cooking, make a mixture proportionately of a tablespoon of salt, ½ teaspoon of freshly ground black pepper, 1 teaspoon cloves, and ½ teaspoon powdered ginger. Dust the birds liberally with this. Then strip with thin slices of salt pork.

Set breast side up in a roasting pan. Arrange a layer of wild mustard (*Brassica*) leaves over the birds. If these are not available where you live, substitute some other peppery wild edible, such as water cress. Roast in a hot 425° oven for 15 minutes or until tender. Then remove both the leaves and the slices of salt pork, brush with melted butter into which a little lemon juice has been squeezed, and brown.

Breast of Partridge

This leaves you with a lot of other portions for soup, but the latter can be good, and the over-all effort is well worth the trouble. Brown the breasts from 4 partridges with ½ stick of butter in a large frypan. Then add the contents of a large can of sliced mushrooms, juice and all. Cover and cook in a moderate 325° oven for ¼ hour or until the meat is tender.

In the meantime, cook enough rice, preferably wild, for 4 people according to the directions suggested in Chapter 6.

In a separate pan, bring a pint of heavy cream and ½ cup of fine sherry to a simmer. Then remove this from the heat and thicken it by slowly stirring in 2 beaten egg yolks into which a small amount of the hot liquid has first been mixed.

Spread the hot rice in a pan. Arrange the partridge breasts

on top. Spoon on the mushrooms. Pour the cream sauce over everything. Sprinkle lightly with grated Parmesan cheese. Then brown under the broiler. Your gourmets will be more than ready by this time.

Partridge and Rice

Start to sauté ½ cup of chopped onion in ½ stick of butter over low heat. Stir in ½ cup of chopped water cress and continue to cook until the onions are tender but not brown.

Then add a cup of stock in which the giblets have been simmered, 2½ cups of fluffy cocked rice, and the boned and cubed meat of a roast partridge. Salt and pepper to taste. Heat until all the moisture has been absorbed.

Remove from the heat, stir in a beaten raw egg, and frost with the contents of a small package of slivered almonds that have been browned in butter. If you weren't hungry when you started, you will be by the time everything is ready, especially if the nostalgic shriek of appetite-stimulating wind is being scratched on the black quiet of the night.

Cold Partridge Sandwiches

These are superior for an informal lunch when you have several cold roast partridge. For the utmost in flavor, do not slice the birds until ready to eat. The other ingredients you'll need are a liberal supply of garlic toast, especially some made from crusty sourdough bread. Let everyone serve himself.

For the odds and ends of meat that will be left, mix with enough gravy to moisten, add a few chopped nuts such as freshly gathered hazelnuts or walnuts, season to taste with celery salt, and spread between thin slices of well-buttered bread.

Trading Post Pasties

A hearty meat pie is hard to beat—and they know this at the fur trading posts spotted throughout northern Canada where this receipt, adaptable to many different game birds, has been handed down by generations of bewhiskered cooks. It hasn't lost a bit of flavor in translation. The following pasty, geared in this instance to partridge, is one of the reasons.

Sift together 2 cups of flour and 1½ teaspoons of salt. Cut in ½ cup of shortening, using two knives or a pastry blender, until the mixture resembles corn meal. Add ¼ cup of finely chopped beef kidney suet. Gently stir in a small amount of water, preferably ice cold, 3 or 4 tablespoons, depending on the absorbency of the particular flour. Place the dough in the refrigerator to chill.

Mix together 3 cups of boned and chopped cooked partridge, ¼ cup diced onion, 1 cup diced raw potato, ½ cup chopped parsley, ¼ teaspoon freshly ground black pepper, and finally a teaspoon of salt.

Roll the pastry out on a floured surface. Then cut it into 4 large squares. Spoon ¼ of the filling on ½ of each square, filling a triangle. Moisten the edges with water, fold the empty triangle over the filled portion, and crimp with flour-powdered fork tines to make a tight bond. Prick the tops with a fork to allow the steam to escape.

Place the four pasties on a cookie sheet or shallow pan and bake in a preheated hot 425° oven for 45 minutes or until the crust is an appetizing brown. These are best direct from the oven. If any last, they also are memorable with cold lunches.

Quail

When you are fortunate enough to have them, rub 4 of the little delicacies—carefully picked and wiped so as to keep the juice conserving skins as intact as possible—with a moderate amount of salt and freshly ground black pepper. Brush with melted butter.

Heat a stick of butter and a tablespoon of olive oil in a deep, heavy skillet. When this mixture is hot, set in the birds and rapidly sear all over. Then pour a cup of sherry and the juice of one orange over them, cover, and cook the toothsome quartet at a reduced temperature until a sharp fork can be easily inserted and withdrawn.

Place on a warmed platter and keep hot until you can bring the remaining liquid to a simmer, correct the seasoning with salt and freshly ground black pepper, and pour it over the fowl. Then douse the quail with ½ cup of heated brandy, Metaxa for a taste treat. Set afire. Serve immediately and better make certain that the provider's shell supply is sufficient for more wing-shooting excursions.

Camp-Style Quail

If, like many of us, you get hungrier than usual when the first chill shiver of autumn crisps the wind, and the dogs start to stir more restlessly, sauté enough onions to go around in a liberal supply of butter in the frypan, cooking them over low heat until they are tender. Then add the quail, split down the back and flattened.

Cover and simmer until tender, turning at about the halfway point. Season lightly to taste with salt and pepper and serve with the hot sauce. This is really something when the trees close to the lodge cast thick, dark shadows over the shakes and little puffs of breeze rattle through rustling grass, already sere and frostbitten.

Roast Quail

Rub each quail with salt and melted butter, cover the breasts liberally with strips of salt pork, and roast in a hot 400° oven for 20 minutes or until tender. Brush frequently with melted butter. About 5 minutes before the fuming little fowl are done, take off the pork strips so as to bronze the breasts. Garnish with water cress and serve on toast, along with chopped giblets which have been simmered in a savory broth.

If you live where the coveys are thick, vary the above recipe on occasion by stuffing each quail with 1 or 2 oysters and a lump of butter. Another subtle flavor variation can be effected by sprinkling each quail inside and out with crushed tarragon leaves, after you have applied the salt and melted butter.

Broiled Quail

Split each quail along the backbone with a sharp knife and flatten it. Rub with salt, freshly ground black pepper, and, if you want it, a little thyme. Start the broiling with the bony side nearer the heat. Baste frequently with melted butter, turning and browning until tender. As always with quail, eat immediately. With the light of early dusk streaming from one patio to another, like hands clasping across the shadowy green spaces between, these'll taste like ambrosia.

Quail in Sour Cream

This recipe both successfully overcomes quail's dryness and complements the fragile flavor of these birds. With 4 quail, melt 2 tablespoons of butter in a large frypan. Sauté the four-some that have been well wrapped with toothpick-pinned salt pork, turning them as they brown.

Crush ½ dozen juniper berries, put them in the pan with the quail, pour a cup of boiling water over everything, and simmer until the tiny fowl are tender, adding more hot water whenever this should become necessary. Salt and pepper to taste. Then add a cup of sour cream, ¼ cup of sherry, and bring to a simmer.

Roast Pheasant

This need not be the tough, dry, tasteless offering so often served the dejected gunner. Rub the young bird inside and out with butter, adding a tablespoonful to the cavity, and dust lightly with powdered marjoram. Lard the breast liberally with salt pork strips. Roast in a moderate 325° oven for 45 minutes or until tender, brushing every dozen minutes with melted butter. See if you don't agree that this is a savory way to combine the contrasting variety of pleasures of both the civilized and the wild places.

Broiled Pheasant

A very young pheasant, split down the back and broiled, can be a long-remembered delight. Rub with butter, salt and freshly ground black pepper mixed 4 to 1, and a little tarragon. Start the flattened bird with the bony side nearer the heat and broil for 12 to 15 minutes, brushing frequently with melted butter. Turn and finish broiling skin side toward the heat 8 to 10 minutes, or until the juices run clear yellow when the meatiest portions are pierced deeply with a fork. Serve on hot toast that is yellow with butter.

Braised Pheasant

Melt ½ stick of butter in a baking dish atop the stove and turn a pheasant about in it until the bird is well bronzed. Then remove the fowl long enough to sauté a diced medium-size onion until soft but not brown. Add a cup of sliced mushrooms and spoon these about until they are nearly done. Stir in ¼ cup dry sherry, ½ teaspoon salt, and ⅛ teaspoon freshly ground black pepper.

Cover the breast of the pheasant with strips of salt pork, return it to the dish, and relegate to a moderate 350° oven for an hour or until tender, basting with the pan juices several times. Thicken the gravy if necessary, garnish with water cress, and serve hot, perhaps with wild rice and a crisp green salad. This will really give a new warmth to that terrace nook.

Young Pheasant with Cream

Disjoint two young pheasants, putting the backs and wings aside for soup. Season with freshly ground black pepper and salt. Sauté in ½ stick of butter in a frypan until lightly browned. Then cover with a pint of heavy cream, add ¼ cup of dry sherry, and simmer until the pheasant is tender and the sauce has thickened. This repast really deserves wild rice.

Old Pheasant in Cream

This recipe will deliciously subdue a large pheasant, cut into serving pieces except for the back and wings, which can be later combined with the giblets for soup—started by covering the entire bird with water and simmering for 20 minutes.

For the main dish, rub the pieces with salt and freshly ground black pepper, brown lightly in butter, and move to a well-buttered casserole. Add 3 tablespoons of butter including the juices and melted butter from the saucepan, 3 tablespoons of dry sherry, 2 cups thick cream, and salt and pepper to taste. Cover and cook in a slow 300° oven for about 2 hours or until the meat is tender. Serve with hot rice, preferably wild.

Pheasant with Water Cress

Start with the chopped water cress, briefly simmering 2 compactly packed cups of this in a cup of water, seasoned with ½ teaspoon salt, until tender. Then drain it well. That way you can use the vitamin- and mineral-teeming water in cooking your bird. Incidentally, you'll want about a pound of pheasant per person.

Cut the pheasant, which may be the grandfather of the flock, into serving pieces. Rub each with lemon juice and then salt. Dust with freshly ground black pepper and with cloves. Brown slowly on all sides with a stick of butter in the bottom of a roasting pan.

Then add the water from the water cress, a cup of heavy cream, and if you want it, ½ cup of good dry sherry. Cover tightly. Cook in a slow 325° oven for about an hour or until the meat is tender.

Move the bird to a warm platter. Add the water cress to the gravy and mix until all bits of the greens are well coated. Then spread over the pheasant and serve. For an added touch, arrange small squares of toast, fried in butter, along the rim of the platter and top each with chopped giblets. See if you don't agree that the intriguingly different flavor is as refreshing as the cool silver shock of a plunge into a stream's living water.

Pheasant Hash

When you've served roast pheasant and some is left over, here's a way to resurrect it that retains all the delicate flavor of this nobleman among game birds. Cut the meat into about ¼-inch cubes. For every cup of fowl, stir in ½ cup of light cream. Cook, along with a tablespoon of butter for every cup of poultry, until the cream warms and thickens. Season to taste with salt and with freshly ground black pepper. This is the sort of fine food that evokes so many praises.

Roast Wild Goose

Wild geese, which should be drawn promptly after shooting, will be the better for being stuffed with a sliced lemon and a chopped onion overnight before cooking. Then remove this stuffing. Rub the bird inside and out with 4 parts salt, 1 part freshly ground black pepper, and 1 part allspice. Stuff loosely with also later discarded slices of onion and apple in equal parts. Truss. Crisscross the breast with bacon and put other slices over the wings and legs. Roast in a slow 300° oven for at least 2 hours.

Wild geese, unlike their less active domestic brethren, tend to be dry and need frequent basting with melted butter. If the honker is of doubtful age, help things along by pouring a cup of sherry into the pan and covering for the last hour or so of cooking.

If the leg joints move easily when pressed with a clean cloth, the bird is nearly ready for the table. All that remains is to bronze the skin. Raise the oven heat to 350°, remove the bacon slices, and baste liberally with the pan juices once or twice during the next 10 to 15 minutes.

Gravy may be concocted with the drippings and giblets, although I prefer to save the livers to make pâté. If any of this roast goose is left, it makes excellent sandwiches, particularly if you spread the bread with some of the cold gravy instead of butter, and bring out the taste of the bird with slivers of sweet pickle.

Older Geese

There's nothing like showing some respect for age, and this axiom applies admirably to an aged honker. You'll spot him by his thick, coarse plumage and the heavy, long-exercised spurs. No oven-roasting for this old-timer! After being hung for a bit, the bird should be simmered in a savory broth until tender, then used in a change-of-pace casserole.

Just cut the most readily available meat into strips, using the remainder for soup. Brown this meat in a frypan with a stick of butter, seasoning it to taste with salt and freshly ground black pepper.

In the meantime, start the cleaned and diced heart and gizzard simmering for ½ hour in a cup of white wine, ⅛ teaspoon celery seed, and salt and freshly ground black pepper to taste.

When the meat is browned, move it to a well-buttered casserole. Remove the cooked heart and gizzard to the hot frypan, reserving the liquid in which they were cooked. Stir them around in the butter until the bits are bronzed. Pour in the cooking liquid and stir vigorously over a moderate flame to loosen all the brown particles in the frypan. Then pour everything into the waiting casserole.

Add a dozen tiny onions and a cup of shredded carrots. Stir in sour cream to cover and set in a slow 325° oven until the vegetables are tender, about ½ hour. Sprinkle with paprika, and open an alley to the table.

Wild Goose Pâté

Sauté the livers, preferably in goose fat until soft, which takes only a few minutes. Add an equal volume of eggs that have been hardcooked by being kept simmering, completely covered by water, for 15 minutes.

Mash to a paste. Then season to taste with salt, paprika, a few flakes of freshly ground black pepper, and a bit of grated onion. If the resulting paste seems too thick, thin it with a spoonful of fat drippings. It is especially tasty on thin, hot toast.

Stewed Pigeon or Dove

It is the practice to refer to the larger members of the family *Columbidae* as pigeons and to the smaller ones as doves.

The meat of both is dark in color and delectable of flavor, varying considerably in different regions according to the quality and quantity of food. "Pigeons" in particular have a tendency to be tough. Unless your birds are young and reasonably plump, it is sound practice to simmer them, tightly covered, in a small amount of salted water or tomato juice either atop the heat or in a slow 300° oven from 30 to 45 minutes or until just tender.

Or, for a brace of these delicacies, dice 4 slices of bacon. Place this in a flameproof casserole along with ½ stick of butter and ½ cup of diced onion. When the onions have started to tan, put in the two birds, a clove of finely chopped garlic, ⅛ teaspoon thyme, a bay leaf, and the drained contents of a small can of mushroom caps.

Stir over a hot fire until the birds are well browned. Spoon off excess fat. Then pour in 2 cups of sauterne, cover, and simmer until the meat is tender. Thicken the sauce with a little butter and flour that has been kneaded together and serve steaming hot. This is a dish that quickly gains your reverence.

Sautéed Pigeon or Dove

These are such delicious morsels, especially if you are lucky enough to have young and tasty birds, that even those who customarily settle for eating one will probably be reaching for the second.

Strew the fowl with sifted flour, salt, and a few flakes of freshly ground black pepper. Brown them in butter, turning them so they'll cook evenly. Then, while they are still spluttering, sprinkle with tarragon and continue turning and cooking until they are tender. Serve immediately, enhanced with their own juices which may be stirred for a minute in the hot pan with a little fine sauterne. The aroma as well as the taste will be heavenly.

Potted Dove or Pigeon

Sometime when you're having another couple over for dinner, cut 4 large pigeons or 6 doves into pieces, rub well with butter, salt liberally, speck with a few flakes of freshly ground black pepper, and sauté briefly in 6 tablespoons butter. When the fowl has taken on a tempting tan, move to a casserole.

Add to the hot butter remaining in the pan ½ cup of chopped onion and ¼ cup of chopped celery. Cook, stirring, until the onion is soft but not brown. Then pour in a cup of boiling water in which a chicken bouillon cube has been dissolved, or use chicken or similar stock. Add a small can of pieces and stems of mushrooms, the juice included. Mix thoroughly, then turn everything over the birds. Cover and cook in a moderate 350° oven for about an hour or until the meat is tender.

Unless you have wild rice for this, try stirring and cooking 2 cups boiled rice in 2 tablespoons butter in a frypan over low heat for 5 minutes. Add 2 tablespoons chopped, preferably green, onions. Cook several minutes longer. Then add a beaten egg and stir vigorously until the egg is set. Season with parsley flakes and salt. Serve everything hot. This will really set off the arriving night when the pale saffron glow overhead begins to fade into velvet darkness.

Roast Pigeon or Dove

If you have cooked wild rice with which to stuff these tidbits, this can make all the difference. In any event, rub the birds well inside and out with salt and freshly ground black pepper, mixed in proportions of 4 to 1.

Roast uncovered in a moderate 325° oven for 45 minutes or until tender, brushing every 10 minutes with melted butter. This, if you like—and you owe it to yourself to try it at least once—may be mixed with an equal amount of sauterne. As with all cooking, so little of any wine is used that this is no department in which to try to save money. Serve the birds hot, doused with steaming juices. This is the sort of food that brings fond memories and nostalgic sighs.

Broiled Snipe

Some natives esteem the stomach contents of such animals as the caribou, for such greens, mixed as they are with digestive acids, are not too unlike salad prepared with vinegar. Other aborigines do not bother to open the smaller birds and animals they secure, but pound them to a pulp which is tossed in its entirety into the pot.

Likewise, many gourmets prefer such game birds as snipe and woodcock cooked with the intestines left inside. These entrails are afterwards removed, chopped, mixed with butter and perhaps wine or brandy, and spread on toast.

If you want to try broiled snipe this way, pluck the birds, but do not draw or even open them. Rub them well with butter, salt, and a little freshly ground black pepper. Broil them not too close to the heat for about 25 minutes, turning them frequently so as to cook them evenly. Season to taste. Serve on crisp buttered toast with or without the chopped intestines.

Roast Snipe

Pluck, clean, and draw the birds. Rub well inside and out with butter, salt, and a little thyme or allspice and freshly ground black pepper. Crisscross the breasts with thin strips of salt pork. Roast in a hot 400° oven about 25 minutes or until done, brushing with melted butter every few minutes. The results come close to gastronomical voodoo.

Woodcock with Cream

Woodcock, which are similar in appearance and habits to the snipe, are satisfyingly prepared by the same methods used with the preceding gourmets' delight. See if you don't agree that both game birds have a savor that cannot be equaled by any other fowl, wild or domestic. If you can manage it, you should allow a pair of these morsels to each diner.

Woodcock, too, retain their delicacy when cooked with cream, especially if they are protected against losing their juices by being carefully dry-plucked, then drawn through a small slit made above the vent. The tiny liver and heart, along with a tablespoon of butter may then be inserted within the bird which should be skewered shut.

Rub the birds well with butter, salt, freshly ground black pepper and freshly grated nutmeg. Place in a low baking dish and pour 2 tablespoons heavy cream over each bird. Bake in a 375° oven for about 25 minutes, or until tanned and tender, basting every 5 minutes. Spoon the hot cream and juices over each serving. The results will be distinguished.

Fried Woodcock

Another way to cook woodcock without drawing them is by dry plucking birds shot that day, rubbing them with salt and freshly ground black pepper and perhaps a bit of tarragon, and lowering them carefully into a pot of deep oil that is seething at about 365°. After they have tossed and bobbed for 6 minutes, the viscera will have tightened into a clean hard ball that can be discarded, along with the well-picked bones, while heart, liver, and perfectly cooked meat are enjoyed to the utmost.

Crow Breasts

Tasting like chicken with savory overtones of duck, the dark meat of the crow is well worth eating. If you've too many for deep freeze and for friends, even when proffered under the more alluring name of rook, why not feast on the breasts?

Sprinkle each with salt and freshly ground black pepper. Melt a liberal amount of butter in a preferably heavy iron frypan and heat it as much as possible without scorching. Put in the breasts and cover. Lower the heat to moderate and cook about 7 minutes until brown on one side. Then turn and bronze the other.

Add a cup of sherry, re-cover, and simmer until the meat is tender, adding more wine if necessary. Then move the breasts to a warm place. Spoon off all possible fat. Bring the wine and juices to a bubble, stirring and scraping, and add a tablespoon of heavy cream to bind and thicken. Pour over the meat and serve. By this time the air will be permeated with the fragrant promise of wonderfully good things to eat.

Crow with Rice

You'll need about 4 pounds of crow for this dish which will serve four hungry people. The older birds in the bag will do. Cut them into pieces. Brown them for 5 minutes with a stick of butter, 2 tablespoons parsley or a small bunch of water cress, and a large diced onion.

Then add a large can of tomatoes and ⅛ teaspoon cloves. Simmer until the meat is tender, salting and peppering everything to taste. Spoon this over individual portions of hot, steaming rice.

Wild Giblet Soup

Perhaps before you get around to eating your wild fowl, you can make good use of the giblets. Prepare the gizzards by cutting to the hard center and pulling this sac away from the meat. Then cut them into pieces. Carefully disengage the bitter little gall bladder from the liver, cutting away any part of the latter that is left with a greenish tinge. You may also include the wings and neck. For four servings of soup, start with a combination of these ingredients weighing 1 to 1½ pounds.

Place everything in a kettle along with 4 cups of water. Add 1 sliced onion, a stalk of chopped celery, 1½ teaspoons salt, and ¼ teaspoon freshly ground pepper. After 20 minutes, remove the livers and set aside. Continue to simmer the remainder until the gizzards and hearts are tender.

Strain the liquid into another kettle. Add ½ cup wild rice which has been soaked for several hours in cold water to shorten the cooking time. Simmer until the rice is tender.

In the meantime, disengage the neck and wing meat from the bones and skin. Add it, with the chopped giblets, to the rice. Bring everything to a simmer, along with a jigger of sherry. Correct the seasonings if necessary. Then strew with paprika and serve. This has all the heady tang of autumn.

Roast Wild Turkey

This prince of the game birds, one of the most prized of all trophies, has a delicious wild flavor that sets it far above the domestic Thanksgiving fowl. Incidentally, because of feeding practices, you do not find this flavor in the so-called wild turkey from game farms.

Wild turkey, though, because of these same eating and living habits, are leaner and tougher than the domesticated varieties. So as to offset this, and at the same time to enhance rather than diminish the natural savor, you won't go wrong in first steaming your bird for ½ hour over moderate heat with a quart of water in a closely covered roaster Then, shifting the fluid to a handy pot, dry the bird with clean toweling.

Rub with salt and with at least 2 sticks of butter. Place in the now dry and uncovered roaster in a hot 400° oven and brown. Then lower the heat to a moderate 325° and roast until tender, which won't take as long as otherwise because of the initial steaming. Baste frequently with the water from the steaming process and with the melted butter.

For the gravy, stir enough flour, previously mixed to a smooth thin paste with double its volume of cold water, with the juices and the remaining stock over low heat until it bubbles to a rich deliciousness. Such wild turkey is something long to be eulogized, especially when the wind suddenly has teeth in it and there's enough snow in the night to make sequins in the starlight.

Ovenless Turkey

If you have to cook your wild turkey without the benefit of an oven, which may be the case in camp, there's still a way to conserve that wonderful flavor, also ideal for the home patio. Cut and disjoint the bird into serving portions. Rub the pieces with salt and with a very generous amount of butter.

Lay on a large, doubled rectangle of heavy aluminum foil and wrap, crimping all edges securely. Place on a grill over glowing coals or in the edge of a small campfire.

Cook 1½ hours, carefully turning the packet every 20 minutes to insure that every part will be evenly cooked and basted. When the supreme moment for unwrapping arrives, take care to save the juice. This should be distributed in cups, so each feaster can punctuate an occasional forkful of steaming meat by immersing it in the engaging savoriness.

Chapter Three

Small Game:
Food for a King

THE WAY SNOW WAS STEAMING at the fringes of my fire, while trees snapped and ground boomed in the deepening cold, did nothing to detract from the best feed of small game I've ever eaten, indoors or out. Then, too, there was an aquamarine sky alive with the aurora borealis and the companionship of my Irish wolfhound pack dog, all conducive to healthy appetite.

Your hunger would have been really something, too, if you'd spent the better part of a British Columbia day following fresh grizzly tracks. Spring had come late to the Peace River mountains that year, but day after day of melting chinook breezes had blown in. Frigid northeast winds suddenly undercut these in the frosty blueness of late afternoon. Snow began to granulate and crust beneath my feet. Finally, I saw where the big bear had paused for a backward look, then lifted its walk to a lope, and I turned back to where I had cached my small outfit.

Ordinarily, I'd have settled that night for beans, bacon, and bannock. But I had earlier crossed the trail of a friend who was out beaver trapping, and he'd given me a plump, young hindquarter. I browned this on both sides in its own fat, sprinkled chopped onion over it while still forking it around, and salted and peppered it. Then I tipped in enough hot water from the boiling kettle to cover the bottom of the frypan, slid on a lid, and eased the whole thing to where enough birch coals were glowing apart to keep it simmering while I made camp.

Particles of heavying frost had started to drift downward in the subzero stillness when, about an hour later, my fork slipped easily into the sputtering quarter. Helped along with gravy-dripping baking powder biscuits, and sluiced down with mug after mug of seething black tea, that meat was delicious.

Incidentally, this is one of the same ways I cook beaver on a city range, perhaps proving that some of the most delectable dishes in the world are of a pristine simplicity, while still boasting an elusive savor beyond the most elaborate continental concoctions.

Trees, ice, and ground were cannonading with cold when I finally dropped off to sleep. But what brought me awake, twisting in my eiderdown, was the drip of water. It was chinooking again. The remaining beaver proved moist and tasty in sandwiches that day and the next. By the time it was gone,

I was sitting down to a feast of grizzly liver and not much else. But happily!

Fresh, plump meat is the single natural food that contains all the nutritional ingredients essential for mankind's good health. Neither anything else, not any particular portions, need be eaten. Savory roasts, if that is what you prefer, will furnish you with all the nourishment needed to keep you robust even if you eat nothing else for a month, a year, or a decade.

One way to accomplish this in gourmet fashion during these days of high prices? By not passing up the small game that is freely available to many of us, often throughout the entire year, and which in numerous cases, as when there is a woodchuck shooter in the family, if not eaten will only be wasted.

Much small game is considerably more of a treat than deer, moose, caribou, and their ilk because of its fat. For this same reason, beaver, opossum, and such should be used within three months, when frozen, as fat does not keep well. On the other hand, the lean rabbit will retain its fine texture and flavor for up to a year. Otherwise, handle, package, freeze, and store small game according to the general directions given in the chapter on big game.

What can the sportsman of the family hunt where? The best way to get the current answer is by writing to the game department in the capital city of the state or province in which you're interested. Possibilities differ widely.

License requirements vary, too. So do the added incentives of bounties. Among the states in which these latter have long been available are: Alaska, Arizona, California, Connecticut, Indiana, Iowa, Kansas, Maine, Massachusetts, Michigan, Missouri, New Hampshire, New York, Ohio, Rhode Island, South Dakota, Utah, and Vermont.

One tip, at any meal! Try to have enough of everything for seconds.

Roast Beaver

The dam-building beaver provided greater incentive for the exploration and development of this continent than any other animal. Lured by their thick glossy pelts, trappers ventured deeper and deeper into wild country, to be followed by pioneers seeking new homes. Explorers traveled farther and farther into the North American wilderness in search of fresh beaver cuttings, and towns strung along their trails.

Moist dark beaver meat, which tastes and smells like Thanksgiving, roasts up particularly well, especially if you have a small, tender trophy. With older beaver, if you prefer to cook them this way, it's best first to treat the meat with a tenderizer as suggested in the chapter on big game, as otherwise the flesh will become more and more stringy the longer you try to tenderize it with heat.

The most effective procedure is to trim off any excess fat and to keep grease from accumulating in the pan. Be preheating your oven to a moderate 350°. Cut small slits in the meat and insert slices from a clove of garlic. Rub the beaver with a teaspoon of rosemary. Sprinkle with salt and freshly ground black pepper.

Place on a rack in a shallow pan and roast, uncovered, until a sharp fork can be easily inserted and withdrawn. And don't worry if you have more than everyone can devour at one sitting. Cold, roast beaver remains moist and flavorful.

Beaver Tail Soup

Dry oven heat will cause the scaly dark skin of these flat appendages, which Vilhjalmur Stefansson included among this continent's five greatest delicacies, to puff and lift away in sections, exposing a fat, white, gelatinous meat. The way I've come to enjoy this best is in a thick pea soup, good enough to make an innocent think he is eating his way across France.

Place 2 quarts of cold water, 2 cups of split peas, and a small, skinned, cut-up beaver tail in a large kettle. Bring to a boil and skim. Then add a large chopped onion, a cup diced celery, ½ cup diced carrots, ⅛ teaspoon thyme, and a bay leaf.

Simmer 2 hours or until the meat separates from the bones. Remove the beaver from the soup. Discard the bones and the bay leaf.

Either press the vegetables through a sieve or puree them in an electric blender. Return the meat and vegetables, along with the liquid, to the kettle. Season to taste with salt and freshly ground black pepper. Bring again to a simmer and ladle out piping hot.

Beaverburgers

If you come by a so-called blanket beaver, an adult so named because its large pelt was accepted as the standard in trade by the 300 year-old Hudson's Bay Company, which once owned all beaver-rich western Canada, beaverburgers may be the solution. They are sumptuous.

With 2 pounds of ground beaver meat, lightly mix a medium-size diced onion, a small diced tomato, a teaspoon salt, ¼ teaspoon freshly ground black pepper, ½ cup chopped water cress, ½ cup newly made croutons, ¼ teaspoon basil, and ⅛ teaspoon marjoram. Divide 4 portions and gently flatten.

Sprinkle a thin layer of salt over the bottom of a heavy frypan and set over high heat. As soon as the salt begins tanning, add the steaks. For rare, which are tastiest, cook a total of 2 minutes on each side.

Otherwise, cook until satisfactorily browned on one side, turn, brown the other side, then lower the temperature and cook until an inquiring fork indicates that your burgers are done to taste.

Baked Rabbit

This is excellent when you have some young rabbits and the time. It has enlivened more than one table, hand-hewn and otherwise. Divide the animals into serving pieces. Salt each and place, bony sides up in a roasting pan. Sprinkle with paprika and cover generously with chips of butter.

Bake, covered to keep in the moisture, in a moderate 350° oven for 1½ hours, turning the pieces and shifting them from top to bottom as they brown. Then transfer to another pan and return to the oven to keep warm.

In the meantime, be simmering the livers and hearts in water so as to end up with ½ cup of stock for each rabbit. Again for each rabbit, add a tablespoon of sifted flour to the butter and juices in the roaster. Stir until smooth. Then add the stock and, mixing and heating, make gravy. Season to taste with salt and freshly ground black pepper and transfer to a gravy boat. Serve everything without delay. When you eat rabbit like this, there seems to be a heavenly chorus singing in the foreground.

Fried Rabbit

This is my favorite way of cooking America's most hunted game. Divide the rabbit or hare into serving pieces, disjointing whenever possible. Dip each portion in milk. Salt and pepper, and then roll lightly in flour.

Put ½ stick butter and 4 tablespoons cooking oil in a frypan over high heat and set in the pieces, any bony sides uppermost. Lower the temperature at once and cook, uncovered, until the portions are brown on one side. Then turn, just once, and brown the other side. The meat will be crisp and done in a total of slightly more than ½ hour. Spread it out on absorbent paper and keep warm while concocting the gravy.

For this, pour off all the fat except just enough to cover the bottom of the frypan. Stir in 2 tablespoons flour, ½ teaspoon salt, and ⅛ teaspoon freshly ground black pepper, smoothing it into a paste. Using the milk into which you dipped the meat, add enough additional milk to make a cupful. Pour this, then a cup of water, slowly into the pan, all the time stirring. Simmer over low heat for 12 minutes, adding more milk and water if the gravy becomes too thick. Finally, sprinkle with paprika and parsley flakes. With everything served hot, the gravy has enough distinctiveness to transmute fried rabbit into an art form.

Oven Rabbit

Having lived in wilderness where salt-hungry snowshoe rabbits were so thick that they once dropped a shelter onto my occupied sleeping bag by gnawing the guy ropes, I can testify from personal experience that rabbit is one of the most versatile of the free foods. Here's a variation that is welcome after you've been getting along for a few days on fried rabbit.

Divide your animal into serving portions. Mix a teaspoon

salt, ¼ teaspoon freshly ground black pepper, and ⅛ teaspoon tarragon. Rub this into the meat. Then brown ¼ pound of diced salt pork in a frypan. Sauté the pieces in this until they are golden.

Chop up a large onion and spread it over the bottom of a baking dish. Pour the contents of the frypan over this. Add ½ cup of water and 1 tablespoon of vinegar. Cover tightly and bake in a slow 275° oven for 2 hours. Try this with highbush cranberry jelly. The combination will delight even the most seasoned of gourmets.

Rabbit and Split Peas

Put a rabbit that has been divided into serving pieces, ¼ pound diced bacon, 2 medium-size diced white onions, and a pound of fast-cooking split peas into 2 quarts of cold water. Bring to a bubble and keep simmering for about an hour or until everything is tender. Season to taste with salt and freshly ground black pepper. Give a final stir and dish out immediately. This has been a universal favorite wherever we've served it.

"Jugged" Hare

This is an ancient dish, especially popular in England, and the recipes differ. Here's one that's both easy and good. Using perhaps a handy casserole, brown a rabbit or hare that has been divided into serving pieces in a liberal amount of butter, at the same time seasoning the meat with salt and freshly ground pepper.

Pour over a cup of claret and add enough boiling water, in which 2 chicken bouillon cubes have been dissolved, to cover the rabbit. Add a large onion stuck with 2 or 3 cloves, a tablespoon lemon juice, a bay leaf, a teaspoon of thyme. Cook, covered, in a slow 275° oven for 3 hours.

Before serving, remove the onion and bay leaf from the cooking liquid and set the rabbit pieces aside to keep warm. Knead together 3 tablespoons butter and 3 tablespoons flour. Stir this into the hot stock and simmer, stirring constantly, until the gravy is smooth and thickened. Then add ¼ cup claret. When the rabbit is removed to a hot deep platter, this gravy may be poured over the succulent pieces.

Rabbit Stew

Fresh mushrooms, peas, carrots, and onions go so well with America's most popular game animal that you may care to try rabbit stew. Cut your rabbit into serving pieces. Brown these in butter in which a diced onion has been cooked until soft. Season to taste with salt and freshly ground black pepper and with ½ teaspoon each of rosemary and thyme. Then half cover with hot water, put on the lid, and simmer 1½ hours or until the meat is tender. Add your idea of enough sliced young carrots, sliced mushrooms, and fresh peas. Continue simmering until these are done.

Then melt 2 tablespoons butter. Mix in 2 tablespoons

flour, ¼ teaspoon salt, and a few flakes of freshly ground black pepper, making a smooth paste. Thicken the stew with this, simmer 5 minutes longer, and serve hot, garnished with parsley flakes or water cress. Such a feast is tempting with the faint familiar odor of the peas and carrots, the authority of onion, the hearty fragrance of mushrooms, and the artful, earthy lure of the meat itself.

Rabbit and Noodles

Melt a stick of butter in a large frypan. Chop a large onion and brown it in the butter until soft and golden. Slice a pound of mushrooms, add them, and tan lightly.

You'll need about 2 cups of cooked rabbit, boned and cubed. Add this to the contents of the frypan, along with a teaspoon salt and ½ teaspoon paprika, and heat until warmed through.

Then sprinkle 2 tablespoons of flour, ⅛ teaspoon thyme, and ⅛ teaspoon rosemary over everything and stir until thoroughly blended. Pour on 2 cups of sour cream. Simmer until thick. Serve over hot buttered noodles. This will establish you as an artist of the skillet.

Rabbit with Sherry

This is tasty for a change. Divide your rabbit into serving portions. Brown these in 2 tablespoons apiece of butter, shortening, and bacon drippings in a frypan over low heat.

Then pour off all but enough grease to cover the bottom of the pan.

Chop a small bunch of water cress into fine bits. Mince a clove of garlic. Combine these with ⅛ teaspoon thyme and ⅛ teaspoon rosemary. Add to the meat in the frypan, along with a finely chopped, medium-size tomato and a cup of sliced mushrooms. Sauté together for 5 minutes, seasoning to taste with salt and freshly ground black pepper. Then add ½ cup of dry sherry, cover, and simmer for about 20 minutes or until the rabbit is tender. This is something to enjoy when just two of you are alone with the crickets and the evening light.

Hasenpfeffer

Varying hare are very thick some years in the Peace River country of northern British Columbia, where we have a log cabin. And speaking of these medium-size rabbits, brings to mind the excellent dish known as hasenpfeffer. I have tried at least a dozen recipes, but the following one is my favorite.

You'll need about 4 pounds of rabbit, divided into serving pieces. Marinate these in a glass or earthenware bowl, for 2 days refrigerated, covered with equal parts of red wine and mild vinegar, 2 cups sliced onions, 6 whole cloves, 4 bay leaves, 2 teaspoons salt, 1 teaspoon freshly ground black pepper, 1 teaspoon dry mustard, 1 teaspoon thyme, and 1 teaspoon tarragon. Turn the meat the first thing every morning and again before going to bed.

Then wipe the rabbit dry, sprinkle with a little flour, and

sauté in a Dutch oven or heavy saucepan with a stick of butter until browned on all sides. Strain the marinade and pour it over the meat. Cover and simmer over low heat for about 40 minutes or until the mildly flavored, finely grained sections are tender. Correct the seasoning with more salt and freshly ground black pepper if necessary.

Serve the rabbit on a hot platter. Add a tablespoon of sugar to the juices. Thicken with a thin paste made by smoothly blending 6 tablespoons of flour with ¾ cup of cold water. Simmer, stirring, for several minutes. Then mix in a cup of sour cream. Bring to a bubble, pour over the rabbit, and serve with steaming buttered noodles. Everything will have a smooth, sensuous taste.

Roast Rabbit

Young rabbit has such a delicate flavor, too often overpowered by other ingredients, that—if you have a rotisserie—you may wish to roast a brace of these until just tender, seasoning them only by brushing them with melted butter every 10 minutes. The result is rabbit pure and unspoiled: succulent, moist, simple, with a fragility of woodland flavor not otherwise obtainable.

If you have no rotating spit, roast the young rabbits in a low uncovered pan in a slow 325° oven until a sharp fork can be easily inserted and withdrawn, again brushing every 10 minutes with melted butter.

Older Roast Rabbit

Cook in a slow 325° oven, adding ½ stick of butter and ¼ cup water to the low, uncovered roasting pan. Place the rabbit on its side in the liquid for 20 minutes, then turn to the other side until tender. Make all the more tempting by spooning the hot water and butter over the meat every ten minutes.

Marinated Rabbit or Squirrel

Soy sauce gives a different and highly agreeable flavor to wild meat, as we discovered one winter in the Far North while living on moose meat and not much else except for the occasional varying hare and red squirrel bagged for the sake of variety. It can really impart that special something to serving pieces of either of these latter, marinated all afternoon in, if you are preparing enough for four: a cup of soy sauce, ¼ cup sherry, 1½ teaspoons sugar, and a minced clove of garlic.

Place the portions on a rack in a shallow pan and roast them uncovered in a preheated moderate 350° oven until tender, brushing them every 10 minutes with the marinade. They'll then be sheer gastronomic delights.

Sautéed Squirrel

Once the prime target of buckskinned pioneers, the numerous squirrel that chatter across the continent still provide gourmet eating, particularly as these small trophies, like rabbit, have little if any gaminess.

The sweet, velvety, short-fibered meat is especially good sautéed. Just cut it into serving pieces. Forking these over frequently, brown them quickly in a liberal amount of butter in a preferably heavy frypan. Then season to taste with salt and freshly ground black pepper, lower the heat, and cook until tender.

Or if this small game is a bit on the mature side, bronze the sections in a stick of butter for ½ hour or until nearly tender. Then cover with hard cider and simmer until this has been absorbed and evaporated. Finally, melt 2 tablespoons of butter and sauté the portions until they are crisp. This is truly a sportsman's dish.

Older Squirrels

Or, particularly if you have a brace of squirrels that are among the elders of their clan, cut them into pieces. Brown these in 3 tablespoons of butter in an uncovered, large, heavy frypan.

Meanwhile, dice ½ dozen slices of bacon and bronze these in another pan, tipping the accumulating fat to one side so the bits can tan more deeply. Then add a diced onion, ¼ diced green pepper, and a cup of chopped fresh mushrooms.

Sauté to a rich brown. Season to taste with salt, paprika, and freshly ground black pepper.

Cascade all this over the sizzling portions of squirrel. Add 3 tablespoons of flour mixed smoothly with a cup of dry sherry. Cover and simmer about an hour or until a sharp fork inserts and withdraws from a test piece of meat without binding, by which time it will whet the most jaded appetite. Serve with bountiful mashed potatoes.

Broiled Squirrel

Split enough cleaned and skinned squirrels for four. Rub them all over with salt and freshly ground black pepper in proportions of 4 to 1, respectively. Melt ½ cup of butter and add ½ teaspoon of thyme and the juice of ½ lemon. Baste the squirrels with this, as you cook them either over glowing coals or under a preheated broiler until tender.

In the meantime, be simmering the livers and hearts in a minimum of water until the latter are tender. Add a cup of heavy cream and ¼ cup of dry sherry. Heat, short of a boil, 2 minutes. Then take the mixture off the stove, slowly stir in a beaten egg yolk, which has been mixed with a bit of the hot liquid, and correct the seasoning if necessary. Move the meat to a heated platter and spread the gravy over it. Serve hot, along with chopped parsley. Such a combination will accomplish wonders, particularly when the nearby yards are dissolving away into darkness and Venus lights her taper in the western part of the sky.

Roast Squirrel

Squirrels well rubbed with butter and roasted uncovered in a moderate 375° oven from 1 to 2 hours or until tender are famous, especially if you brush them with additional butter every 20 minutes. Stuff them first, if you prefer, with chopped onion, celery, and carrot in equal volumes.

Serve hot with gravy made by blending an equal volume of flour with the pan drippings, then stirring in enough hot water to make a smooth gravy. Season to taste with salt, freshly ground black pepper, and paprika.

Brunswick Stew

Cherokee, Chickahominy, and other native Americans kept a pot of stew seething over their small campfires. The leftovers that went into this included squirrel, beans, corn, and tomatoes, assuring an ever-ready repast that the Jamestown colonists came to call Brunswick stew.

Because of the nature of this treat, recipes vary. One I like, geared to a pair of cut-up squirrels, is started by adding to the meat a cup apiece of whole-kernel corn, diced onion, and diced bacon, along with the contents of a defrosted package of frozen lima beans. Bring this to a bubble with 3 cups of water. Simmer until the meat is tender.

Then add the contents of a small can of tomatoes, salt and freshly ground black pepper to taste, and ⅛ teaspoon rosemary. Sauté a cup of soft white bread crumbs in ½ cup of butter and stir this gradually into the stew, along with ½ cup of dry sherry. Serve immediately in flat soup plates. The glory of this stew lies in its lovely, heady savoriness which goes a long way to prove that food can be a lot more than just something to fill that hollow space under the ribs.

Roast Opossum

In addition to a gourmet feast, the rewards of opossum hunting include robust outdoor exertion and the resounding music of hounds.

Although the animal often is roasted with the hide on, I prefer to skin it first, at the same time discarding the glands from the small of the back and beneath the front legs. However, you can scald your trophy for a couple of minutes in very hot water, scrape off the hair with a dull knife, then slit open and clean, saving the heart and liver. I remove both head and tail, although the former is sometimes left on by those savoring the tasty lean strips of meat thus afforded.

Rub the skinned opossum inside and out with 4 parts of salt and 1 of freshly ground black pepper. Stuff loosely with 3 parts diced apples and 1 part seedless raisins. Roast, uncovered, in a slow 300° oven for ½ hour per pound or until tender, basting occasionally with the juices that accumulate in the pan.

A favorite accompaniment is parboiled sweet potatoes, peeled, halved, sprinkled with brown sugar, and placed around the meat the last 15 minutes. The sizzling 'possum fat seeping into these improves even their flavor.

Opossum and Sassafras

Another way to enjoy roast opossum on occasion in sassafras country is to skin it, trim off all but ¼ inch of any excess fat, rub as before with salt and freshly ground pepper, stick the outside thickly with green sassafras twigs, and roast unstuffed as above.

Broiled Opossum

The fine-grained and light-colored meat—the tenderer because of mild-flavored, well-distributed fat—also cooks up exceedingly well above the gleaming coals of a patio grill. Rub the halves or serving pieces with salt, freshly ground black pepper, and a little sage. Broil about an hour or until tender, basting with fresh lemon juice. The air appears to be filled with an enthralling clarity when you bite into meat like this and the flowers seem to be giving off a special scent.

Baked Opossum

This is a good way to prepare large members of the tribe. Simmer the cleaned and skinned opossum in salted water until tender. Then remove, wipe dry, dust with freshly ground black pepper, and set in a shallow baking dish surrounded with parboiled sweet potatoes.

Bake in a moderate 350° oven until a rich brown, basting every few minutes with fat skimmed from the water in which the meat was cooked. Everything will be blended so harmoniously that it will be both elegant and substantially exquisite.

Braised Woodchuck

Woodchuck are very much worth saving, especially if after skinning them you carefully remove the small, kernel-like glands from inside the forelegs. Unless too grizzled and tough, woodchuck are generally best roasted.

If you run into a patriarch, though, brown the pieces in a small amount of butter. Then cover with water, season to taste with salt and freshly ground black pepper, and simmer 2 hours or until tender. Add vegetables such as potatoes, carrots, and parsnips when the meat is nearly done. If any 'chuck is left for serving cold, it will be juicier and more flavorful if allowed to cool in the stock.

Rabbit recipes also make young woodchucks standout attractions in the culinary department.

Woodchuck Stew

An oldster of the tribe will do admirably for this. Simmer in a savory broth until the meat falls away from the bones. Cut this into cubes with a sharp knife or scissors.

Place in a large casserole, along with a quart of the strained stock thickened with 3 tablespoons butter and 3 tablespoons flour kneaded together. Add 2 cups of diced cooked potatoes, ½ cup cooked green peas, ½ cup cooked diced carrots, ½ cup sautéed mushrooms, and ⅛ teaspoon apiece of tarragon and basil. Bring to a simmer. Served hot with steaming baking powder biscuits, this will make the world appear brighter.

Woodchuck Soup

When the 'chuck shooting has been especially productive, soup may be the solution. Place the bones and any odds and ends of meat in a large kettle, cover with cold water, add your idea of enough salt, and simmer for 2 hours until the meat is free of the bones. Strain this stock, cool, and skim off all the fat. Pick out as much of the meat as you can from what's left.

Chop a leafed stalk of celery. Dice 3 medium-size white onions and 3 carrots. Simmer in a small amount of salted water until they are tender and most of the water has been evaporated and absorbed.

Cook a cup of rice, wild if you can manage it, until tender, and then strain it.

Blend 2 tablespoons of butter with 2 tablespoons of sifted flour. Stir this vigorously into the stock, now heating in a large kettle. Add the meat, rice, vegetables, ⅛ teaspoon of marjoram, and salt and freshly ground black pepper to taste. Bring to a bubble, then serve sprinkled with either chopped parsley or water cress. The results will be something over which to grow lyrical.

Cream of Woodchuck Soup

This recipe is so delectable that you may choose to try it using other small game as well. It's a delicious way to utilize the oldsters, as well as odds and ends, simmering them slowly all morning or afternoon in salted water until you have a rich stock. Let this cool and spoon off all the fat.

For enough soup for four, blend ½ stick of butter and ¼ cup of sifted flour over low heat. Cook slowly for several minutes to take away the raw taste. Then gradually pour in 3 cups of the strained broth and simmer, stirring constantly until thickened. Add cubed woodchuck if you wish.

Then pour in a cup of heavy cream and warm the soup until bubbles begin to plop. Do not boil. Season with ¼ teaspoon crushed garlic, 2 teaspoons lemon juice, a coloring of parsley flakes and paprika, and salt to taste. Serve with a liberal scattering of small bread cubes, freshly fried in butter until golden. Few things taste as good.

Sautéed Frog Legs

The texture and flavor of frog legs are not unlike that of white chicken meat, although their taste is even more delicate. The smaller the frogs, the tenderer and sweeter they are. Strip the skin off like a glove. Practically all the meat worth saving, you'll then see, is on the hind legs. Like fish, these are at their tastiest when fresh or when frozen fresh.

For sautéing, they may first be rolled in lightly salted and peppered flour, cracker, or bread crumbs, perhaps after being initially dipped in cream. If you prefer a crusty coating, immerse them between rolling in egg beaten with a tablespoon of cold water.

Sauté in a liberal amount of butter or olive oil for about 10 minutes or until the tender golden brown meat comes away from the bone.

You often can find a little water cress close by whose bite will help bring out the flavor. Tartar sauce and French-fried potatoes are the easiest accompaniments. Sautéed mushrooms also are excellent. Or you may prefer to sprinkle the sizzling delicacies with freshly chopped parsley and bring them out on hot toast along with lemon wedges. On any occasion they provide a worthy adjunct to even the most sumptuous of feasts without attempting to efface the deliciousness of the salad or soup.

Grilled Frog Legs

Frogs, believed to be the first animals to crawl out of water and live on land, still furnish some of the best food found in either domain. The odor of grilled frog legs will make any patio an even more pleasant spot. Dip the tidbits in cream, then in fine cracker crumbs, and broil over open coals for 10 minutes or until tender, turning occasionally and brushing with melted butter.

In the meantime, probably in the kitchen, sauté proportionally, depending on how large an amount of sauce you'll be needing, a small chopped onion in 1½ tablespoons of butter until limp but not brown. Then, stirring constantly, add a teaspoon of flour and cook 2 minutes more. Add a cup of sour cream and a tablespoon of fresh lemon juice. Stirring occasionally, simmer for 10 minutes. Run through a fine sieve, salt and pepper to taste, dust with paprika, and pour hot over the still spluttering frog legs.

Broiled Frog Legs

Brush the frog legs with melted butter, sprinkle lightly with freshly ground black pepper and with salt, set on a rack, and slide 4 inches below the broiler in a preheated oven. After 5 minutes, turn, brush again with melted butter. Cook another 5 minutes or until the meat comes away from the bones.

Serve hot with water cress butter made in the proportions of that suggested in the recipe for Broiled Brook Trout. Few tidbits are as tasty and tender.

Porcupine Stew

"Many campers would pass up a porcupine, on which there is even a bounty in some places, and yet he is the purest of all vegetarians," Colonel Townsend Whelen told me when we were writing our book, *On Your Own in the Wilderness.* "My memory goes back to when Bones Andrews, one of the last of the old mountain men of the breed of Jim Bridger, and I were compelled to spend several weeks in a region where there was no game. At the end of that time we had about the worst case of meat fever you can imagine. So we saddled up our little pack train and made tracks for higher altitudes and game country. On the way up I shot a porcupine. I skinned it, starting at the smooth underneath, and tied it to the back of my saddle.

"That night we made it into a stew. First, we cut it into small pieces and boiled these an hour. Then we added a handful of rice, some salt, a dozen small dumplings of biscuit dough, and covered all that to boil 20 minutes longer. This was tall country. With air pressures lessening with the altitude, the higher you climb, the longer you have to boil. We finally finished by adding a little flour to thicken the gravy and by stirring in a teaspoon of curry powder.

"Then the two of us sat down and finished the whole pot at one sitting. That pot held nine quarts and was full."

Porcupine Liver

The major reason why the porcupine, like the equally uncomely ling, is a gourmet's delight lies in its relatively huge liver. Slice this ½-inch thick. Trim out all the tubes and membranes. Fry a minute to a side with 3 tablespoons of browning butter in a hot frypan.

Then remove the liver to a hot platter, add ½ cup of claret to the pan juices, boil up rapidly, and pour over the slices. Few gustatory experiences will be as rewarding.

On river trips when I've been unable to keep one of the waddling pincushions from gnawing the salt-encrusted gunwales and thwarts of my canoe, I've also relished this liver entwined with sliced bacon and grilled about 4 minutes over the hot fringes of a small gleaming fire.

Roast Coon

Indians up the coast in Maine were hunting raccoons before the first Pilgrim stepped ashore at Plymouth. Not only was the long, warm fur prized, but the savory flesh, not unlike the dark meat of chicken in texture and flavor, was highly relished.

Remove the excessively bitter, bean-shaped, kernel-like scent glands from the muscles under the front legs and each thigh, trim off the sometimes strongly tasting fat if you prefer, and crisscross with strips of salt pork. If someone particularly objects to the flavor of the remaining fat, or if the animal is old and tough, parboil your coon first for ½ hour in salted water.

Roast coon, which takes some 3 hours in a slow 300° oven, is superb, especially if the well-barded little animal is basted every half-hour with the drippings. When nearly tender, remove the pork strips and lightly sprinkle with flour to provide a crisp crust. Continue to baste until the coon is golden brown and tender.

For a particularly tasty gravy, shift the coon to a pre-warmed platter and keep hot in the oven. Skim the fat from the remaining drippings. Then, placing the pan over low heat atop the stove, stir in 6 tablespoons butter, 2 teaspoons powdered onion, and a teaspoon of chopped parsley. Blend in 3 tablespoons of flour and stir until smooth. Slowly stir in 3 cups of hot chicken broth and simmer, stirring constantly until all the rich brown particles in the pan have been incorporated and the gravy is smooth and thickened. Check the seasoning, adding salt if necessary. Raccoon roasted this way will really make your mouth tingle.

Roast Muskrat

When I first smelled muskrat roasting in a Hudson's Bay Company home kitchen in the Far North I thought we were going to sit down to turkey. Nor was the moist, dark meat of the two muskrats that soon were ensconced in the center of the dining room table in any way a disappointment. Four of us were at that dinner, and little was left of the musquash but bones.

If you'd like to try the same dish, remember first to remove the small glands from beneath the hind and forelegs. Sprinkle the insides of two muskrats liberally with salt and freshly ground black pepper, using more pepper than usual. Fill the cavities loosely with a stuffing made of equal proportions of diced onion, diced apple, and seedless raisins. Blend 2 tablespoons of flour smoothly with ½ stick of butter. Rub this over the muskrats and set them on a greased rack in a shallow roasting pan. Place in a preheated, hot 400° oven.

Roast, turning, until golden. Then reduce the heat to a moderate 325°. Cover the two animals with a single layer of cheesecloth that has been soaked in ½ cup of dry sherry. As the roasting continues for a total of 1½ hours, or until the meat is tender, brush every 15 minutes with melted butter and more dry sherry. The result will be the sort of gastronomic experience that's almost unbelievable.

Muskrat Stew

For a change of pace, again cooking for four hearty diners, clean your brace of muskrats as before and cut into serving pieces.

Tan 8 cubed slices of bacon in a large, heavy frypan. Then do the same thing with a big sliced onion. Add the muskrat and, stirring, sauté it over low heat until well browned. Sprinkle on ⅛ teaspoon thyme. Pour in a cup of good red Burgundy. Cover and continue cooking over low heat for 30 minutes or until the meat is tender. Season to taste with salt and freshly ground black pepper.

Blend 2 tablespoons flour with ¼ cup of cold water and stir it into the liquid. Cook, stirring, another 3 minutes. Then reduce the heat, mix in ½ cup sour cream, bring to a simmer only, sprinkle with parsley flakes, and serve over hot rice. The odor will be so tempting by then that this latter had better be ready and steaming.

Cougar

Among many of the Indians who relied on wild meat, cougar was preferred to all other game including venison. It has no game taste whatsoever.

If you ever have the chance to try some, a good way to start is with a heavy frypan with a lid. Sauté 2 medium-size diced onions in ½ stick of butter until they begin to tan. Then add about 2 pounds of cougar, cut into ½-inch cubes. Stirring, cook this, too, until it takes on a light bronze. Add salt and freshly ground black pepper to taste, a cup of dry vermouth, and enough boiling water to cover. Simmer, with the lid on over low heat for an hour.

In a separate pan, smoothly blend 3 tablespoons flour with 2 tablespoons butter. Add a cup of chicken bouillon, made with a cube if no stock is at hand, stirring to prevent lumping. Chop a tablespoon of parsley and add that to the sauce, along with an equal amount of chopped chives. If you have any, ½ teaspoon of chopped chervil leaves will add an elusive flavor. Simmer all this for 6 minutes. Then add a cup of light cream and bring again to a bubble.

Stir this gradually into the meat mixture, bring back to a simmer, mix in a tablespoon of fresh lemon juice, correct the salt and pepper if necessary, and serve over thick slices of French or sourdough bread which you have just turned into hot garlic toast. And don't be too surprised if someone exclaims this is the best meal he has ever eaten.

Small-Game Ragout

Divide about 4 pounds of small game into serving pieces. As soon as a dozen small white onions brown in ½ stick of butter, remove the vegetables and, stirring, sauté the meat until it is well tanned.

Then push the meat to one side, tilt the pan so that the butter will flow into the unoccupied space, and stir ¼ cup flour smoothly into it. Slowly pour in 2 cups of good red Burgundy, stirring until thick and smooth. Add 2 teaspoons salt, ½ teaspoon freshly ground black pepper, and ½ teaspoon thyme. Mix in the nose-tingling onions and a pound of sautéed sliced mushrooms.

Cover and simmer until a testing fork indicates that the now redolent meat is tender. For that final savoriness, serve with hot rice or noodles and tossed green salad. There's something about such a ragout—its plenitude of judiciously blended flavors, the romance of the game, and its satisfyingly delicate heartiness— that makes it one of the most delicious things to eat ever concocted by man.

Small-Game Kabobs

These are always good. On the patio or in the fireplace, you can really dress them up. For about 2 pounds of any tender small game— rabbit, squirrel, raccoon, opossum, or such— you'll need ½ stick butter, 2 tablespoons lemon juice, ¼ pound sliced bacon, and enough sliced onions, firm chunks of tomatoes, to be impaled through the skin, and mushroom caps to go around.

Cut the boned game into cubes about 1½ inches square. Brush these well with melted butter and lemon juice, and let them stand ½ hour.

Using green sticks, metal rods, or whatever you have, thread loosely in succession a piece of game, sliced onion, 2-inch strip of bacon, chunk of tomato, mushroom, game, and so on, ending up with a chunk of game. Brush with the mixed lemon juice and melted butter. Then sprinkle with salt and freshly ground black pepper.

Broil in the rotisserie or 2 inches above glowing coals until the meat is tender, turning occasionally and basting frequently. These kabobs are best when charred outside and still juicily red inside. Serve with potato chips, pickles, and hot garlic bread. Such a blending will convert these refreshing tidbits into a delicacy that will rate high on almost anyone's list of favorite foods.

Chapter Four

Fish and Its Preparation

WITH MORE THAN 30,000 species of fish to choose from, you have plenty of choice. The main thing is not to overcook your trophy. To emphasize fish's delicate flavor and to keep it moist and tender, heat only until the flesh becomes opaque. As soon as the fish breaks easily into flakes, it is done.

The second thing to avoid? Never soak any fish either at stream or waterside or, after it is cleaned, in the kitchen.

Incidentally, fish odor can easily be removed from hands and utensils by rubbing them briskly with salt, rinsing in cold water, and then washing in hot water.

Broadly speaking, there are five general methods of cooking your catch. The simplest but least effective way is boiling, with much of the juice, flavor, and nourishment being lost in the fluid. However, judiciously poached fish can be mouthwatering. In fact, this latter way of cooking is considered by gourmets to be the most delicate way of preparing fish when done properly; no juice, flavor, or nourishment being lost.

All fish are eminently suited to the frypan. Steaming can be effective, particularly for the leaner varieties whose flesh will remain firmer. Baked fish, especially if frequently basted and if enhanced with a sauce, can merit a place on any table.

When I remember the trout I've cooked over the apple-red coals of outdoor grills, with a bit of the savory juices dripping down on the embers with a hiss and a little dance of flame, I have to pick broiling as my favorite all-around treatment. It is unusually effective with the plumper species whose oily content keeps them from becoming too dry. But with the others, all you have to do is add fat, such as that in a tasty strip of bacon.

Fish, prepared ready to cook, should preferably be frozen the day it is caught, although it can be cleaned and stored in a cool place or dryly packed in ice for a reasonably few days if one is on vacation.

The fatter fish such as lake trout, salmon, and eels can just be cleaned, wrapped apart from one another in meal-size portions in moisture-vapor-resistant coverings—with two layers of waxed paper between individual steaks, fillets, and small fish—and frozen at 0° or colder. These fatter fish should be used within six months, although flavor and texture will be better within three months.

The leaner fish will be the better for first being given a 30-second dip in a solution made by dissolving ⅔ cup salt in a gallon of water. Then drain, wrap, and process as usual.

Lean fish will keep some eight months at 0°.

Frozen fish may be cooked as if fresh, although it will take longer for them to become flaky—the sign that they're done. When fish are to be breaded and fried, and when they are to be stuffed, it will be more convenient to thaw them first to make handling easier. The ideal way to thaw fish is in the refrigerator in the original wrappings. Then cook immediately.

A serving of fish generally is ⅓ to ½ pound of edible flesh. Therefore, with brook trout, a sleek 1-pound beauty will do for each individual. When dressed and boned, this will weigh a satisfactory ½ pound. If it is a big lake trout, on the other hand, and you are serving fillets or steaks, you'll want about ⅓ of a pound per person—unless you are on vacation where appetites are especially hearty.

Fried Trout

Rub salt and freshly ground pepper into your trout. Then dip the steaks, fillets, or cleaned small fish for a moment into evaporated milk. Next, dust bread crumbs over them and fry them in a liberal amount of butter, just hot enough that it has begun to color.

Turn only once, as soon as the first side is brown. The total time depends on thickness. Test with a fork or toothpick. As soon as the trout is easily flaked, it is done. Remove at once to hot plates or a well warmed platter.

Squeeze the juice of a lemon into the pan, add some chopped water cress, stir about a bit, and you'll almost instantly have a noble sauce to turn over your trout as you enjoy it sizzling from the fire.

Oven-Fried Trout

For enough small, whole fish or fillets for four, melt a stick of butter. Pour half of this into a baking dish and warm for 5 minutes in an oven preheated to a very hot 500°.

In the meantime, beat an egg yolk with ¼ cup of light cream. Salt and pepper to taste. Then stir in ½ teaspoon of chopped water cress and ¼ teaspoon paprika. Dip the fish in this before rolling in fine, dry cracker or bread crumbs.

Remove the baking dish from the oven long enough to arrange the coated fish in it. Distribute the remainder of the melted butter over them. Return to the heat for 8 minutes or until the fish flakes readily. Serve immediately, perhaps with lemon wedges to lend a special flavor.

Grilled Trout

The smaller the trout or other fish, the hotter the grill should be. If the fish breaks or sticks when you turn it or take it up, then odds are that you didn't let the metal get hot enough at the onset. Too, grease the grill well at the start.

Either salt the inside and outside of the trout up to an hour before broiling, or sprinkle the inside with freshly ground black pepper and lemon juice just before it goes on the heat. Whole fish may be split or not, depending on the size and on your preferences. Even when the fish has a thick skin well cushioned with fat, brushing frequently with melted butter will add to the flavor. Once the translucency of the flesh has clouded to opaqueness, the fish will be ready for serving.

Paprika butter melted over grilled trout enhances both appearance and flavor. This can be easily prepared beforehand by melting in a skillet, proportionately, a tablespoon of butter, mixing in ½ teaspoon of powdered onion, and cooking over low heat until golden, constantly stirring. Allow this to cool, cream with a teaspoon of paprika and butter, shape into about 1-teaspoon portions and relegate to the refrigerator.

Baked Brook Trout

Another engaging way with brook trout is to bake it to a flaky goodness, each cleaned but otherwise whole small fish, wrapped in 2 strips of bacon. For 6 of these trout, prepare the scene by lightly sautéing a tablespoon of chopped green onion with 3 tablespoons butter in a shallow baking pan. Then put in the catch, slide into a hot 400° oven, and bake until opaque.

Shift the trout to a hot platter. Stir a teaspoon of lemon juice, ½ teaspoon parsley flakes, and salt and freshly ground black pepper to taste into the juices in the pan. Bring quickly to a simmer and pour over the trout. Serve with water cress and lemon wedges. There is a gusto and a sensuous, open-eyed delight to be experienced from food like this.

Baked Lake Trout

For a smooth golden taste with about a 4-pound lake trout, mix a teaspoon of salt with the juice of a large lemon. Rub the trout inside and out with this.

For the stuffing, blend 2 cups of soft bread crumbs, the drained contents of a small can of mushroom stems and pieces, ½ stick melted butter, and a small diced onion. Stir in a teaspoon of very finely chopped celery, ⅛ teaspoon thyme, and a coloring of freshly ground black pepper. Add a tablespoon of brandy and a tablespoon of heavy cream.

Stuff the trout about ¾ full and fasten with toothpicks. Place in a buttered, shallow baking dish and bake uncovered in a preheated moderate 350° oven for about 45 minutes, or until the trout is flaky, basting with melted butter. Any extra stuffing may be baked for ½ hour in a shallow pan. Serve on a hot platter, tastefully surrounded with parsley sprigs and lemon wedges.

Trout Lamé

This can give you some moist, tasty morsels on those days when you are preparing a quantity of small brook trout. Unless you object too strenuously, leave on the heads and certainly the tails where, in that order, lies the sweetest meat. Then salt the cleaned fish inside and out. Lay a sprig of water cress in each.

Chop some mushrooms into small pieces, sauté these in

butter only until soft, and place a tablespoon of the bits along with the melted butter atop each trout. Brush the part of the foil that will be in contact with the fish with melted butter and fold tightly to hold in the moisture.

Place the packages apart from one another in a preheated hot 425° oven and bake for 8 minutes. Then open the foil of each packet at the top, turning it back from the fish. Cook until the flesh flakes easily, watching everything closely from now on, as this takes only moments.

To enjoy these trout at their best, melt another slice of butter voluptuously in a warm streak atop each fish and serve each in its own attached hot plate. They'll then be as welcome as a refreshing spring encountered after a long day's hike in the blazing sun.

Rainbow Trout in White Wine

To go with enough of these small bright fish to serve four, sauté a chopped medium-size onion in 3 tablespoons of butter in a baking pan until soft. Then add the fish, well rubbed with salt and a little freshly ground black pepper. Pour in 1½ cups of dry sauterne. Bake in a hot 400° oven about 12 minutes. As soon as the trout are flaky, transfer them to a hot platter.

Mix 2 tablespoons of flour to a smooth thin paste with 4 tablespoons of cold water and stir this slowly into the wine and juices. Heat atop the stove until thickened. Then mix in ½ cup heavy cream and 2 tablespoons chopped water cress.

As soon as this is seething, pour over the exquisitely waiting rainbows and serve.

Trout Meunière

This classic French cooking method, popular around the fine fishing waters of Quebec, is excellent with small, whole, cleaned fish. With 4 brook trout, for instance, melt ½ stick of butter in a heavy frypan and add 2 tablespoons of good olive oil. Rub salt and freshly ground black pepper into the fish, inside and out. Dip them in heavy cream, sprinkle with flour, and sauté until flaky. Remove to a hot platter.

Without wasting any time, squeeze the juice of a large lemon into the pan, toss a handful of chopped parsley, stir about a minute, and then pour over the trout. Serve immediately. There are books one enjoys rereading and this repast resembles them. You'll find it just as superb the second and third times you taste it.

Spitted Brook Trout

You can enjoy these either beside the stream or on the patio. Slit the fish open and clean them. You can then, if you prefer, rub in a little salt and freshly ground black pepper, but the smoky, slightly charred flavor is going to be so harmonious that seasoning really isn't necessary.

Shove a sharpened, green hardwood stick about a yard long through the mouth and out the tail of each trout. Hold over hot coals, or above the fringes of a small campfire, until a testing twig indicates that the flesh will flake easily.

The fins then will pull out readily, and if you're cooking bass or some other fish that otherwise would have required scaling, you'll find this unnecessary as the hot skin will easily peel, leaving quickly disengaged bones and moist, delicious meat.

Broiled Brook Trout

Rub the cleaned but otherwise whole trout with a mixture made proportionately of 1 part of salt, ¼ part of freshly ground black pepper, and ⅛ part of paprika. Brush with melted butter. Place on a prewarmed buttered pan and slide 4 inches beneath the broiler. Broil without turning for about 8 minutes or until the meat along the backbone flakes easily.

Serve hot with water cress butter made, if you are serving four, by briefly cooking ¼ cup butter, ½ teaspoon salt, ⅛ teaspoon freshly ground black pepper, 1 teaspoon lemon juice, and 2 tablespoons chopped water cress over low heat until the butter starts to tan, by which time everything will be blended in a harmony as meltingly unforgettable as that of a Tchaikovsky theme.

Lake Trout with Mint

You'll often find wild mint (*Mentha*) in dark green stands beside the waters in which you catch lake trout. This can be gathered and taken home, as it will keep indefinitely. For about a 4-pound fish, mix ¼ cup olive oil, 4 tablespoons fresh lemon juice, 3 tablespoons of the chopped mint leaves, ½ teaspoon thyme, and salt and freshly ground black pepper to taste. Brush the trout with this.

Lay the fish on a well-buttered grill and set 4 inches below the heat. Broil until golden and flaky, brushing several times with the spiced oil. Bring the unusual and intriguing results to the table on a preheated platter, garnished with sprigs of mint and surrounded by lemon wedges.

Sautéed Trout

This is hard to beat when it comes to filleted lake trout and to toothsome brook trout. Open and clean these latter as soon as possible after catching, saving the livers, hearts, and any roe, if you can use them immediately. Again, unless someone takes issue too determinedly, leave on the head and tail where, in that order, you'll find the tastiest tidbits. The trout can then be kept frozen at 0° up to 8 months before using.

When you're ready to cook, get the frypan just hot enough so that, if you're cooking for four, the ½ stick of butter in it barely begins to brown. You can roll the trout in flour or crumbs if you wish, although I much prefer the rich crispy skin "as is." Some use corn meal for a coating, too, but to me it has an unpleasant toughening effect.

Brown the fish on both sides, only until the flesh flakes readily. The heart, liver, and any roe will then also be done and tender. Transfer to a hot platter and add any desired salt. You also may like to squeeze on a few drops of lemon juice.

For an excellent sauce, let the pan cool some over very low heat. Then carefully add 2 teaspoons of vinegar, 4 teaspoons of chopped parsley, and, if you wish, 2 teaspoons of chopped capers. Brown all this slowly and pour over the hot fish.

Poached Trout

Use either small trout or serving-size portions. Place in a large frypan. Barely cover with hot milk, tomato juice, or with water lightly salted to taste. Cover and simmer, well short of a boil, for 10 minutes or until the flesh is flaky. Then remove to a hot platter and keep warm.

Blend a tablespoon of flour with ¼ cup of cold milk and add this slowly to the remaining liquid. Bring to a simmer, stir in ½ cup of heavy cream, and heat again to a bubble. Remove from the heat and slowly add 2 beaten egg yolks. Cascade over the hot fish and serve.

Trout with Almonds

Let's face it. The fishing can be too good! Some weeks, both by the shore and later at home, we gorge ourselves so nobly with brook trout and such that the day arrives when we guiltily realize we'd almost rather reach for a plebeian hamburger. When this happens, the following recipe can be a passport to further piscatorial pleasure.

In a small skillet, heat 2 tablespoons butter and toss in 3 tablespoons slivered almonds, bought that way if you prefer. When the nuts are lightly browned, stir in a teaspoon paprika, 2 tablespoons lemon juice, and 2 tablespoons chopped parsley.

Then, in a frypan large enough not to crowd 6 trout, melt 3 tablespoons butter and, when this is hot, sauté the salted and peppered catch over medium heat until their undersides flake readily. Now turn the fish, tip the little skillet of sizzling almond butter over them, and finish cooking.

Poached Atlantic Salmon Steaks

This is one of the ways I've enjoyed these fighting beauties on the *Half Moon* of the Southwest Miramichi River in New Brunswick and later at home in Boston. For enough steaks for four, bring 6 cups of water, 1 tablespoon of vinegar, and 1 teaspoon of salt to a bubble in a large frypan. Add the salmon and simmer for 10 minutes or until the fish is flaky. Serve drenched with melted butter.

Planked Grilse

A grilse, as you may know, is the young of the salmon after its first return from the sea. A delectable way these young Atlantic salmon have been served to me, both on the southwest Miramichi and on the Grand Cascapedia which enhances Quebec's Gaspé Peninsula, has been planked.

Start with a heated, oiled, inch-thick birch plank which can be hewn on the spot. Wipe the cleaned and split grilse with paper or cloth toweling, rub inside and out with salt and freshly ground black pepper in respective proportions of 4 to 1, and broil in a preheated oven at 450° for about a dozen minutes or until flaky, basting with melted butter.

This procedure also brings out the flavor of steaks from freshly caught salmon like no other method I know of. Again, heat and oil the plank. Brown the steaks under the broiler for 2 minutes on each side, then bake them in a preheated hot 450° oven for a few minutes more until they flake easily. Basting with melted butter will add to the flavor.

Sautéed Filleted Salmon

To go with enough fillets for a hungry foursome, break 4 eggs into a bowl. Mix with 1 teaspoon allspice, and 2 tablespoons thick cream.

Then rub salt and freshly ground black pepper, in the proportions of 1 teaspoon of salt to every ¼ teaspoon of pepper, into the fillets and soak them in the well-beaten mixture 5 minutes. Sprinkle with flour. Fry them in ½ stick of butter until flaky.

Remove the fillets to individual preheated plates. Stir in a teaspoon of water cress and the juice of a lemon into the butter in the frypan. Pour over the hot fish. With this flavor so set off and heightened, they can adorn the table of the most fastidious of gourmets.

Poached Salmon

For about 4 pounds of salmon steaks or fillets, start by preparing a court bouillon. You'll want a chopped stalk of celery, ¼ cup diced carrot, a small sliced lemon, 2 teaspoons salt, a sprig of thyme, a bay leaf, and 1 quart of water, although this latter amount will depend somewhat on the size of the fish and the receptacle. Boil for 10 minutes. Then taste and add any necessary salt. Pour in 1½ cups of good dry white wine and simmer several minutes.

Cradle the salmon in cheesecloth, using a large section of this so the ends can serve as handles. Lower into the court bouillon, the heat under which should be lessened until the liquid is barely bubbling. Simmer about 20 minutes or until the fish is flaky. So as not to overcook, test frequently for flakiness. Then lift the salmon carefully out of the bouillon and transfer to a hot platter and keep warm.

For the sauce, bring a cup of light cream, ¼ cup of the strained court bouillon, ¼ teaspoon salt, a coloring of freshly ground black pepper, 2 tablespoons melted butter, and 2 finely chopped hard-cooked eggs to a bubble. Remove from the heat and stir in a beaten egg yolk and a tablespoon of chopped water cress. Serve hot with salmon.

The results will be as savory and as delicate as any you can taste.

Salmon Loaf

It's a common thing in both the Northeast and the Northwest to cook more salmon than you can readily eat. Baked salmon loaf is then often the solution.

With every 2 cups of skinned, flaked, and boned salmon, mix a cup of finely crumbed bread or crackers, a cup of rich milk, a beaten egg, a tablespoon of minced onion, a tablespoon chopped water cress, ¼ teaspoon salt, and a sprinkling of freshly ground black pepper.

Level in a buttered baking pan and bake in a moderate 350° oven for ½ hour or until set. Then cool 3 or 4 minutes in the pan before turning onto a hot platter.

This is good with a rich onion sauce. To make this latter in proportions for the above, melt a tablespoon of butter in a pan, remove from the fire long enough to stir a tablespoon of flour smoothly into the butter, and then return to low heat to bubble—but not brown—for a minute.

Add a tablespoon of grated onion and cook this until yellow and soft. Pouring slowly and stirring constantly, add a cup of heated half-and-half milk and cream and simmer for 10 minutes. Stir in a teaspoon of lemon juice. Then salt to taste. Pour over the hot salmon loaf and start serving. The plates must be very hot.

Smallmouth Bass Salad

The friend who used to serve this salad to us made it with smallmouth bass, caught just outside his island cottage, but like the other recipes in this section, it will work with other fish as well, either frozen or fresh. With every cup of flaked cooked fish, mix ½ cup of finely chopped raw carrot, ½ cup of chopped raw apple, and 2 tablespoons of chopped raw tomato. Salt to taste.

For the dressing, blend 2 tablespoons mayonnaise, ½ cup heavy cream, 1 teaspoon prepared brown mustard, ⅛ teaspoon paprika, and a tablespoon of fresh lemon juice.

Shape the portions on beds of crisp lettuce, flavor liberally with the dressing, and lightly with parsley flakes. This is a distinctive and unusual salad, mingling as it does so many different flavors in concentrated form.

Baked Bass

This recipe is one to reach for when everyone's mouth is watering for something a little different. For a 4-pound bass, mix a teaspoon of salt, ¼ teaspoon freshly ground black pepper, and ⅛ teaspoon apiece of parsley flakes and paprika. Rub the prepared bass inside and out with this.

Distribute the slices from a medium-size onion inside the fish. Lay in a well-buttered baking dish and cover with 6 slices of bacon. Bake, uncovered, in a moderate 325° oven for 45 minutes or until the fish flakes readily.

When the bass is nearly done, make a cheese sauce for it, starting by blending ½ stick of butter with 3 tablespoons of flour. Slowly add this to 1½ cups of milk over low heat, stirring constantly. Then remove from the stove.

When the sauce has cooled a bit, begin stirring in ⅔ cup of good grated Cheddar cheese, putting in only small amounts at a time and mixing vigorously before adding any more. If you want a more decided taste, include ½ teaspoon of prepared mustard. Then return to very low heat, continuing to stir. If the sauce still is not as velvety as you would like, try rapidly mixing in a tablespoon of cognac. Serve everything hot, blended into one delectable savory whole.

Pan-Fried Blue Gills

Dust the blue gills with flour, salt and pepper them liberally, and lay them carefully in a yellow pool of fresh butter in a sizzling frypan. Brown lightly but crisply on both sides over moderate heat until the white flesh flakes easily. Serve with all the butter cascaded over them and with perhaps a little more added.

Baked Pickerel

The firm sweetness of this long, sporty fish lends itself particularly well to baking. Rub lemon inside and outside a pair of 2-pound pickerel. Then salt and pepper.

Arrange in an uncovered shallow pan, with ½ cup of

water, and garnish with water cress and ½ stick of chipped butter. Bake in a moderate 350° oven for 30 minutes or until flaky. About 15 minutes before the fish are done, pour ½ cup of heavy cream over them. To catch all the first fine savor, serve as soon as removed from the oven.

Bullhead Chowder

Not much to look at, but easy to catch and superlative to eat. the bullhead makes an outstanding chowder once it has been skinned, boned, and cut into chunks. The same is true of the firm, well-flavored flesh of the ling.

Using a deep, heavy kettle if possible, sauté ½ cup of cubed salt pork until the bits become crisp and brown. Remove them for the time being.

Slowly sauté a cup of chopped onion in the remaining fat until soft and golden. Add 1½ teaspoons salt, ¼ teaspoon freshly ground black pepper, 3 cups diced potatoes, and water barely to cover. Simmer 10 minutes.

Then add about 3 pounds of skinned, boned fish cut into cubes and continue simmering until this is flaky. Knead 2 tablespoons flour with 3 tablespoons butter, blend into a cup of the hot broth until smooth, then carefully stir back into the kettle. Add 2 cups of milk, check seasonings, and continue to simmer until all is piping hot. Stir the brown bits of pork back in and serve the chowder immediately with crackers. This is enough for four.

Arctic Grayling Omelet

Again, any fish may be used, but this is the way we make this omelet in my cabin up on the headwaters of the Peace River. For two hungry diners, drench 2 cups of flaked, cooked grayling with 2 tablespoons of lemon juice.

Then separate 5 eggs. Beat the yolks. Stir in ½ cup rich milk, 1 tablespoon chopped water cress, ½ teaspoon salt, and ⅛ teaspoon freshly ground black pepper. Mix in the fish. Fold in the stiffly beaten egg whites.

Melt 2 tablespoons of butter over low heat in a large frypan and sauté 2 tablespoons minced onion until soft. Pour in the egg mixture. Cook over low heat about 10 minutes, until delicately tan on the bottom. Then place in a preheated slow 300° oven for another 10 minutes or until the top is firm. Divide and serve on heated plates.

Eels

The French Jesuits who early canoed up the St. Lawrence River and its wild tributaries found the Indians enjoying eels, often broiling them over campfire coals on green sticks, a method still to be recommended today. The trick with eels in most methods of cookery is to leave the skins on, which then act as protective coverings to keep the meat succulent and juicy.

First, scour the elongated fish with a brush or, if you're outdoors, with a handful of wood ashes. Then cut into convenient pieces, 2 or 3 inches long, and clean them by twisting a fork or such through the hollow. Wash, rub with salt, and brown with a liberal amount of butter in the frypan until flaky. If this is your first experience with eel, no fish will ever taste better, and you'll never eat more.

Broiled Eel

Eels are even better broiled. For about a pound, which ordinarily will serve two, mix ¼ cup olive oil, the juice of a lemon, and a tablespoon of chopped water cress. Immerse the pieces prepared as above in the liquid. Salt and pepper sparingly.

Put in a shallow baking pan and place 6 inches below a preheated broiler. Cook for 5 minutes. Then season with the remainder of the oil mixture. Continue broiling until the fish flakes readily. Serve on hot plates, garnished with additional water cress and with lemon wedges.

Fish Balls

For some fine food that will evoke many praises, mix 2 cups of flaked, cooked fish with 4 cups of mashed potatoes. Stir 4 beaten eggs, ½ stick of melted butter, 1 teaspoon salt, and ¼ teaspoon freshly ground black pepper into the mixture. Form into ovals about the size of golf balls, drop into deep fat, and let fry for about 5 minutes or until brown.

For the bacon that is good with these, dip the slices into 2 eggs beaten with ⅛ teaspoon Worcestershire sauce. Roll in cracker dust. Melt 2 tablespoons butter in a warm frypan, add the bacon, and sauté until golden, turning once.

Drain on paper toweling and serve piping hot, along with tartar sauce and the still sizzling fish balls. At the first mouthfuls everyone's discontent will begin to vanish like smoke, and a most joyous enthusiasm will succeed it.

Fish Loaf

This will give you a change, particularly when you're eating your way through a big catch, either fresh or frozen. Bone the raw fish. For each pound, run the fish through the meat grinder with a medium-size onion.

Mix a tablespoon melted butter, 1½ teaspoon salt, ¼ teaspoon freshly ground black pepper, 1 egg, ½ cup of fresh bread crumbs, and ½ cup milk. Add this to the fish and onion and beat until fluffy. Pour into a buttered pan, top generously with slivered almonds and chipped butter, set in a pan of hot water, and bake in a moderate 350° oven for 45 minutes, or until set.

Fisherman's Respite

Fisherman's Respite is for that moment when you feel that tomorrow you may be sprouting fins. Melt ½ stick of butter in the frypan. Add 2 cups cooked, cold, diced potatoes and ½ cup diced onion. Cook slowly, turning everything gently and often until it is lightly browned.

Pour on 3 tablespoons good dry sherry and bring to a boil. Then add 2 cups of flaked cooked fish. Cook a minute or two to warm through; then lower the heat.

Mix ¼ cup whipping cream, 2 slightly beaten eggs, ¼ cup shredded sharp Cheddar cheese, ½ teaspoon salt, ⅛ teaspoon freshly ground black pepper, and ¼ teaspoon tarragon. Stir into the fish mixture. Cook, turning with a spatula until the egg mixture is slightly set, and serve your hungry quartet with this welcome change of pace.

Ling Liver

The greatest delicacy among the free foods, Dr. Vilhjalmur Stefansson, the explorer, always avowed to me, is ling liver. Ling aren't the sportiest fish within casting distance of our cabin site, but these fresh-water cod, which scientists call living fossils, certainly more than hold their own against the Arctic graylings and the rainbow when it comes to eating.

The lings' tastiest parts are their large, fat, vitamin-replete livers. Mostly, I ease on the frypan when coming up from the river, melt a little butter, and briefly sauté them—all the while hoping that no stranger will wander into sight until we have devoured them on the spot. There are times, I'm sure even my friend Stef would have agreed, when you can overdo the companionship bit.

Chapter Five

Shellfish You Will Enjoy

ALONG THE BRIGHT New England beaches, women of the Penobscot and Narragansett tribes dug pits above the high-tide marks in the sand, lined them with stones heated in roaring fires, alternated layers of soggy seaweed and live shellfish, and invented the clambake, still enjoyed in similar fashion by hundreds of families today. You also can relish one of these rousing repasts in your patio or backyard.

For these versions, a huge iron kettle, such as once might have served as a witch's cauldron, can sometimes be picked up for a dollar or two at a roadside antique shop. It need not be intact to hold a seething, savory, scrumptious backyard or patio clambake.

Pack a layer of wet kelp, commonly shipped with these seashore delicacies where they are not otherwise available, in the bottom of this or any other large boiler or kettle. Atop this place a live lobster for everyone. Cover with more damp seaweed. Add enough potatoes in their jackets to go around. Press on more seaweed. Then come such standbys as unhusked corn, seaweed, a bountiful layer of live clams, and a final thick topping of more wet kelp. A lid, which may be an old bit of canvas, is added to seal in both the heat and the wonderfully fragrant steam.

Set or suspend this container over a flaming fire or a bed of hot coals. After about 1½ hours, the cover is removed and the top layer of now dry weed forked out. By the time the clams have been savored with melted butter, the corn should be ready for enjoying with more butter and a bit of salt. Then come the potatoes, with butter along with salt and a strewing of freshly ground black pepper, and finally the lobsters and a replenished supply of liquid yellow butter.

The shellfish proper include the numerous juicy clams, as well as all the oysters, all so excellent on the table both raw and cooked. There are the toothsome scallops. There also are the mussels which enhance the ocean and even the fresh-water varieties, so prized in Europe, making them available for the securing to almost all Americans.

Among the crustaceans as such that are free for the taking are the Pacific's lordly abalone, the skittering crabs that even a child can catch, and the ubiquitous crawfish that, again, thrive in both the inland's fresh waters and the ocean's crashing brine. Then, perhaps to stretch a point, there is the waddling turtle, once so prized in the American kitchen that there were laws limiting the number of times a week it could be fed to slaves.

Shellfish, as a generic whole, have the additional boon of being rich in nutritive values. An average portion affords nearly all the animal protein you need each day to help build and replenish body tissue. Besides providing essential vitamins, shellfish are valuable sources of iodine, copper, iron, calcium, and phosphorus.

This wonderfully free food also is wealthy with built-in variety. Shellfish fit into every meal—breakfast, luncheon, dinner, supper, and snack—and into every course from appetizer all the way to dessert. You can serve this wonder nutriment every day without risk of monotony and for any occasion: family meals, company dinners, parties, picnics, and rousing seashore barbecues.

These delicacies are happily at home in the freezer, a particular advantage since some are available only during short periods of the year. Nutritious and superbly delicious, they are well worth the trouble and time needed to store them this way. Being exceedingly low in fat, properly prepared and packaged shellfish can be well kept at 0° for up to six months, although you'll better appreciate the flavor if you bring them to the table within half that time. If the shellfish is cooked before freezing, it should be used within a month as otherwise it will become unpleasantly tough.

Clams, as well as oysters and scallops if you have them, are first washed as free as possible of sand, then opened and the carefully saved juice strained. Remove all dark portions from the meat. Then place the shellfish in glass jars or other waterproof rigid containers. Cover completely with their own juice, adding 2½ percent brine—made by dissolving ⅓ cup of salt to a gallon of water—if this is necessary. Leave ½ inch expansion space at the top of the container. Then close and seal.

Live crabs, lobsters, and crawfish should be cooked for 20 minutes in 2½ percent brine. When cool, the edible meat is picked out, all membrane and bits of shell being removed from this. The meat is then tightly packed in glass jars or rigid waterproof containers and covered with 2½ percent brine up to within ½ inch of the top. Again, close and seal.

As with all meat, slowly thaw these fruits of the seas and streams for the finest flavor. Then use without delay.

Quick Clams

Maybe you're too hungry to wait that long to enjoy your freshly dug clams. Then just let a fire burn down to coals. Lay your clams directly on these. As soon as they have opened, dip each in melted butter and wash down with cautious sips of their own shell-caught juices.

The same delectable effect can be achieved indoors by laying the clams in a shallow pan and sliding them into a pre-heated hot 450° oven, where they'll soon be steaming in their own juice.

Steamed Clams

You'll probably want at least a couple of dozen clams for each diner. Scrub these first with a stiff brush and wash until they are reasonably free of sand. As always, any clams whose shells do not clamp shut when they are handled should be discarded.

Place the clams in a deep kettle, with about ¼ inch of lightly salted water in the bottom. Cover tightly and steam over moderate heat until the shells partly open. Depending on the fire and the size of the bivalves, this usually takes no more than 10 minutes. Serve at once with melted butter and cups of the rich, salty broth.

For a subtle touch that seems to bring out the savor of the sea, try adding a clove of garlic to the boiling water. You also can touch up the butter by adding a squeeze of lemon juice to each portion. But steamed clams are one delicacy that most of the time I prefer plain.

Mussels prepared the same way also are unforgettable.

Clam Chowder

Nothing's better on a cool, foggy day. Separate the hard necks from the soft, plump bodies of a quart of shucked and cleaned clams. Let these necks simmer ½ hour, or until tender, in a cup of water.

Add a bay leaf, a teaspoon salt, ⅛ teaspoon thyme, and ⅛ teaspoon freshly ground black pepper to a quart of milk.

Simmer a cup of diced potatoes and ½ cup of diced onion in this until they are barely tender.

Then stir in all the clams and liquid, a cup of heavy cream, and a cup of fine sherry. Simmer for 5 minutes. Dust with paprika and ladle out piping hot for four hungry clam diggers.

Baked Clams

Shuck 3 cups of clams, saving the shells. Grind the meat coarsely. Then stir it with 3 eggs, ½ cup of a robustly flavored grated cheese, 1 teaspoon salt, and ¼ teaspoon freshly ground black pepper.

Melt a stick of butter in a frypan over low heat. Stirring, cook ¼ cup of diced onions and a similar amount of chopped celery until they start to soften but not to brown. Then sprinkle on 3 tablespoons sifted flour and continue cooking until the raw flavor has gone. At the same time, bring 2 cups of rich milk to a simmer in a separate utensil. Add this now, and stirring until everything is thick, cook another 3 or 4 minutes.

Stir the contents of the frypan with the clam mixture. Apportion among the clam shells. Sprinkle each with a little more grated cheese, some paprika, and parsley flakes. Add a dab of butter. Bake in a moderate 375° oven for 10 minutes, and have any guests all primed, as these should be enjoyed piping hot.

Clam Pie

Growing up on the New England seacoast, I began to enjoy clam pie early. Recipes for this substantial dish vary considerably, but the one I prefer is heavier on the bivalves than on the accompanying vegetables.

Shuck and clean a quart of clams, always saving the liquor. Dice a large onion and 2 medium-size potatoes. Add enough rich milk to all but 3 tablespoons of the clam juice to give you a quart of liquids. Bring everything to a simmer in this.

In the meantime, cube ¼ pound of salt pork. Keeping most of the fat poured off, fry this over low heat until it is brown and crisp. Then add to the other ingredients. Season with salt and freshly ground black pepper to taste. Keep simmering until the potatoes are just short of being done.

Turn into a large, fairly shallow casserole and top liberally with paprika and parsley flakes. Cover with a rich crust made by sifting together 1½ cups of flour and 1 teaspoon salt, cutting in ½ cup of well-chilled butter, and then gradually adding the 3 tablespoons of remaining clam juice to make a ball of dough.

Roll this out, fit over the dish, press the edges to the rim, prick to make steam vents. Any leftover pastry may be cut into decorative shapes, brushed with beaten egg, and placed atop the crust. Bake in a preheated hot 450° oven for 15 minutes or until the top is golden brown. Serve immediately on hot plates. All the work of preparation will be more than overbalanced by the excellent taste.

Fried Clams

I have boyhood memories of smelling these for miles along the traffic-clogged Massachusetts shores of Essex, Ipswich, and Gloucester, and I still don't know of any odor more conducive to hearty eating. Dry your shucked and cleaned clams. Dip each in beaten egg. Then roll in fine dry crumbs. Fry in deep, hot fat only until golden brown.

Tenderness depends on not cooking these too fast or too long. Drain on paper toweling. To my way of thinking, these are the best after being swirled a bit in tartar sauce.

Clam Cakes

Mix each cup of ground clams with a beaten egg, tablespoon of grated onion, ¼ cup of cracker or bread crumbs, ¼ teaspoon salt, and a dusting of freshly ground black pepper. Pat into thin cakes about 3 inches across. Sauté with butter in a frypan, turning until light brown on both sides. Serve hot, perhaps with quartered dill pickles. By this time, the aroma will be something wonderful.

Grilled Clams

Immerse in melted butter, roll in seasoned powdery cracker crumbs, and grill until golden over cherry-red charcoal or under the broiler. These are treats both to the eye and the appetite.

Angels on Horseback

Drain 2 dozen oysters and marinate them for an hour in the juice of 4 lemons, given additional character with ⅛ teaspoon cayenne pepper. Then dry them, sprinkle lightly with salt, loop ½ slice of bacon around each, and fasten with a tooth-pick. Outfit each guest with a skewer and let him broil his own angels for 3 minutes over the glowing coals of a patio brazier. Or arrange them on a rack in a shallow pan and bake them in a very hot 500° oven for the same length of time.

In the meantime, fry a dozen slices of thinly sliced white bread in a well-buttered frypan. Drain on paper toweling. Serve the sizzling Oysters on the toast, with fresh water cress on the side to add zest and tang to the already exciting repast.

Mussels treated the same way also become tasty tidbits.

Broiled Oysters

As H. H. Munro remarked, "There's nothing in Christianity or Buddhism that quite matches the sympathetic unselfish-ness of an oyster." Maybe he'd just devoured a dozen of the freshly broiled bivalves.

If you'd like to react for yourself, salt and pepper your oys-ters sparingly. Sprinkle with flour. Arrange them on a buttered rack and, turning them when necessary, and brush-ing with melted butter, grill until crisp and tan on both sides.

While this is going on, prepare your sauce by mixing in a pan over low heat for every dozen oysters: 2 tablespoons butter, 1 tablespoon dry sherry, 1 teaspoon lemon juice, ½ tea-spoon cayenne pepper, and salt to taste. Transfer the sizzling oysters to a warm platter and spoon the hot sauce over them. Serve immediately with toothpicks.

Oysters Beverly

Move the liquor and mollusks from the shells to a saucepan. For every dozen oysters, add 2 tablespoons of dry sherry. Simmer the oysters in this for 2 minutes. Then remove the shellfish, add a cup of heavy cream, and cook well short of boiling until the mixture thickens.

Add to the oysters a tablespoon of fresh spinach that has been cooked and drained well, a small white onion, 3 medium-size mushrooms, and ⅛ teaspoon nutmeg. Chop all this together very thoroughly. Cook over low heat, stirring for 5 minutes. Then season to taste with salt and cayenne pepper.

Beat 2 egg yolks and stir them into the other ingredients. Spoon everything into the oyster shells and sprinkle with paprika. Set on a rack. Bake in a hot 450° oven until brown. Serve hot with wedges of lemon. These will stir even the most lackadaisical appetite.

Minced Oysters

For a pint of shucked oysters, melt ½ stick of butter in a pan. Chop the oysters coarsely and add these, along with 2 well-beaten eggs. As soon as this begins to bubble, stir in a cup of bread crumbs, ¼ cup grated Parmesan cheese, a teaspoon salt, ½ teaspoon dry mustard, and ⅛ teaspoon cayenne pepper.

Fill the shells, sprinkle with bread crumbs, top with chips of butter, and bake in a hot 450° oven until the minced oysters brown. No matter how many times you've served these before, they'll still be a gustatory experience.

Scalloped Oysters

For a meal for four, drain 2 cups of the shucked shellfish. Get 3 cups of bread crumbs. Butter a casserole.

Now spread a cup of the bread crumbs over the bottom of the casserole. Lay half of the oysters atop these. Top with ½ stick of melted butter, a sprinkling of parsley flakes and paprika, and cayenne pepper and salt to taste. Go through the same procedure again with crumbs, oysters and seasonings.

Roof everything finally with the last cup of crumbs mixed with ⅓ cup of grated Parmesan cheese. This will give you 3 strata of crumbs and 2 of oysters. Bake in a preheated hot 450° oven for 15 minutes, and don't be surprised at the compliments.

Baked Oysters

"Smells are surer than sounds or sights to make your heart-strings crack," said Rudyard Kipling, who used to live in New England, and he might have been thinking of the aroma arising from baking oysters.

Dip each cleaned oyster into beaten egg, then roll in cracker or bread crumbs. Place on the deeper half of the shell. Dot with butter. Sprinkle with a mixture, proportionately, of 2 tablespoons grated onion, ½ teaspoon salt, ¼ teaspoon paprika, and ⅛ teaspoon freshly ground black pepper. Bake in a hot 425° oven for 10 minutes or until the edges of the oysters start to curl.

Baked Crabs

If the time ever comes when you tire of crabs plunged live into salted boiling water, then seethed 15 minutes before being cracked open and enjoyed with melted butter and perhaps a bit of lemon juice, the following promises a savory change. Coarsely grind 3 cups of cooked crab meat. Mix with 3 eggs, ½ cup of grated mild cheese, ½ cup of good dry sherry, a teaspoon salt, and ¼ teaspoon freshly ground black pepper.

In a frypan over low heat, melt a stick of butter and stir in ¼ cup chopped green onion and a similar bulk of chopped green pepper. When these have started to soften, sprinkle on 3 tablespoons of sifted flour and cook thoroughly.

Then blend the two mixtures. Level in a well-buttered

casserole. Top with a little more grated cheese, a scattering of sliced butter, and a liberal strewing of paprika. Bake 12 minutes in a moderate 375° oven. Serve directly.

Crab Newburg

Melt a stick of butter in a double boiler. Stir in 3 cups of freshly cooked crab meat and cook directly over low heat for 5 minutes. Add 2 tablespoons of sherry, ½ teaspoon paprika, ½ teaspoon salt, and ⅛ teaspoon nutmeg, and place over hot water.

Beat 5 egg yolks with 1½ cups of light cream. Add this gradually to the crab meat mixture, stirring for about 4 minutes or until everything is thick and smooth. Serve immediately on hot wedges of toast to the delighted gourmets.

Crab Meat Salad

Even the widely used mayonnaise is really too strong a dressing for crab meat salad, overpowering too much of the delicate flavor. A small amount of fresh lemon juice and a sprinkling of salt is all you need. Other ingredients? I like crisp fresh lettuce, several chopped, hard-cooked eggs, and perhaps a little diced celery.

Crab Cakes

The flavor of mashed potatoes blends well with the delicate taste of cooked crab meat. Mix a cup of each, along with a beaten egg, ½ teaspoon salt, and ⅛ teaspoon freshly ground black pepper. Mold into cakes. Sauté with butter in a heavy frypan over moderate heat, turning when golden on one side. Drain briefly on paper toweling, and serve hot.

Freshwater Crayfish Bisque

Maybe the day will come when you tire of eating these little crustaceans after boiling them until bright red in a small amount of lightly salted water, then peeling each and discarding the intestine which may be removed by breaking off the center tail fin. If so, try some of this savory bisque.

First, boil down the tasty stock in which 2 cups of crawdads were boiled until ½ cup of liquid remains. Mix this, along with a cup of medium cream, with 2 cans of condensed tomato soup. Season with ⅛ teaspoon oregano and freshly ground black pepper to taste. Then mix in ½ cup of fine dry sherry and, for that extra flavor, a jigger of preferably Metaxa brandy.

Heat to a simmer only. Stir in the cooked, peeled, and cleaned crayfish. Continue bubbling until the little tidbits are warm all the way through. Dust with parsley flakes and serve hot with buttered toast wedges.

Crayfish Patties

Skin divers often come up with large ocean crayfish. If you have access to any of these, cook them by any lobster recipe. Or if you'd like some distinctive patties, take about a pound of the shelled meat. Sauté it with a stick of butter over low heat until tender. Then salt and pepper to taste and chop the crayfish coarsely.

Now cut a stick of butter into 2 cups of flour that has been sifted with 4 teaspoons of baking powder and ½ teaspoon of salt. Quickly work in enough milk to make a firm dough. Roll about ¼-inch thick. Cut into rectangles.

Without wasting any time, spoon generous portions of the cooked crayfish on one half. Fold over the other half and press the edges of the dough together. Place on a shallow pan and bake in a preheated hot 425° oven 15 minutes or until the pastry is appetizingly golden. These are best hot from the oven.

Fried Mussels

Mussels, widely available in both fresh and salt water, afford considerably more food than a similar amount of clams or oysters because their shells are so thin. One of the tenderest and most delicate of shellfish, mussels can be deliciously cooked in all the ways oysters and clams are prepared. If you live along the California coast, though, be sure to avoid them when they are quarantined from May to October because of their eating a plankton poisonous to humans during that period.

All you have to do to prepare mussels is scrub them well, preferably with a wire brush and either pull off the beard (the stringy piece connected to the inside of the shell by which they cling to rocks), or cut it off with the point of a small, sharp knife. Don't use any that stay opened when handled. Incidentally, if you steam your mussels and any have remained closed, discard these without opening them, as the shells will be filled with mud.

For temptingly fried mussels, briefly steam them with a small amount of water in a covered pot until they open. Then discard all black parts, and if you haven't already bearded them, do this now. Dip in beaten egg. Then roll in either fine cracker or bread crumbs that have been salted and peppered to taste. Fry very lightly in butter until a creamy golden yellow.

Mussel Bisque

If you're serving four, you'll want about 2 quarts of mussels in their shells. Scrub these under running cold water, steam them with ½ cup of water in a large covered pot until they open, remove from the shells, discard all black portions, and chop.

Make a paste in the top of a double boiler by mixing 3 tablespoons of sifted flour with a little cold milk. Then gradually add a full 3 cups of milk, stirring everything together smoothly. Heat 10 minutes until the mixture thickens.

In the meantime, peel and quarter enough fresh ripe tomatoes to fill 3 cups. Add a bay leaf and ⅛ teaspoon of basil. Stew slowly about 10 minutes or until the tomatoes are tender. Remove from the heat and add ½ teaspoon baking soda. Strain.

Slowly stir the hot tomato puree into the hot milk. Then, continuing to stir, add the mussels. Season to taste with salt and freshly ground black pepper. Heat thoroughly, not boiling, and apportion at once, decorating each intriguing serving with a tablespoon of eye-catching whipped cream.

Simmered Mussels

Prepare and steam the mussels the same way. Then place them in a casserole, cover with the strained hot broth, add a liberal amount of butter, season to taste with salt and freshly ground black pepper, dust with paprika, and bring quickly and briefly to a simmer. Serve, steaming hot, along with the seething butter and juices, with crusty garlic bread.

Mussel Soup

Scrub a quart of mussels and remove the beards. Place in a large kettle along with a cup of dry sherry, a finely chopped small white onion, a finely chopped small carrot, a finely chopped small stalk of celery, a mashed clove of garlic, a teaspoon salt, and ¼ teaspoon cayenne pepper. Cover and bring slowly to a bubble. Simmer several minutes, only until the mussels open. Overcooking will toughen these, so remove them immediately from the kettle and place in a warm place.

Meanwhile melt ½ stick of butter in a saucepan. Stir in 3 tablespoons of sifted flour. Then pour in a small amount of the fluid from the stock bit by bit, mixing until everything is smooth.

Beat 2 egg yolks with a cup of light cream and add this. Keeping the temperature well below a boil, gradually stir in the stock. Simmer 10 minutes. Then add the mussels and 2 tablespoons of well-chopped parsley. Stir until thoroughly mixed and serve. Try hot, crusty buttered toast with this repast, pleasurable proof of *Homo Sapiens'* ingenuity in transforming necessity into an art.

Abalone Steaks*

The picturesque abalone in its mother-of-pearl shell is a widely sought prize of the cool northern Pacific from Alaska down western North America to Mexico's Baja California. Once you've pried the muscular univalves from rocks at low tide, scoop them out of their bright shells with the same large screwdrivers or tire irons.

Trim off all soft and all dark sections, slice the white meat into steaks about ⅓-inch thick, and pound these with a mallet, hammer, or bottle until soft. Abalone vary in size, and you'll usually need several to give you enough steaks for two.

Editor's note: Since the original publication of this book, the harvest of abalone has been severely curtailed by government agencies. Check with state wildlife authorities before attempting to gather abalone.

Marinate these steaks in a cup of dry sherry and the juice of a fresh lime for 15 minutes. Then wipe dry. Dip into 2 beaten eggs, then into cracker crumbs seasoned to taste with salt and freshly ground black pepper. Get some butter to the point where it is just changing color in a frypan. Put in the steaks and fry no more than a minute on each side. The abalone's distinctively delicate flavor then can be enhanced with a little more lime juice.

Fried Abalone*

Prepare the abalone as for steaks, but then cut each slice in cubes small enough to serve impaled attractively on toothpicks. Shake them in a paper bag with sifted white flour.

Now stir the yolks of 3 eggs together with a fork. Beat the whites and set aside for a moment. To the yolks add a tablespoon of melted butter, a cup of milk, a cup of flour, a teaspoon of salt, and finally 1½ teaspoons of baking powder. Stir briefly and quickly, then immediately fold in the beaten egg whites.

Without any waste of time, immerse the floured abalone bits in the batter and fry in deep fat heated to 375° only until light gold. Overcooking will result in toughening.

A particularly good sauce in which to dip these hot cubes, each on its individual toothpick, can be made by chopping either tender young dandelion leaves or water cress nearly to a paste, then stirring this with an equal bulk of cold mayonnaise. They'll then fill both stomach and soul with a satisfaction not too easy to attain.

*See note on page 153.

Broiled Scallops

Swirl the rinsed and dried scallops in melted butter which has been flavored with lemon juice. Sprinkle with powdered parsley. Place on a preheated broiler pan about 3 inches from the heat and heat until they are a subtle and voluptuous gold, turning them so they will cook evenly.

Sautéed Scallops

Rinse and dry the scallops, quartering them if they are too large. Then dip in lightly beaten egg. Roll in bread crumbs that have been seasoned with 4 parts salt and 1 part freshly ground black pepper. Turning them occasionally, sauté in butter for 2 minutes or until they begin to brown. Sprinkle with chopped parsley and cook until colored a bit more. Eaten hot, these will be gastronomic delights, not merely just another seafood.

Turtle Stew

Some day, when you are seized with a fever for fine eating, scald a turtle, that has been killed by concussion or by decapitation, for several minutes by dropping it into boiling water. The under shell may then be quartered and the entrails removed, whereupon the meat can be readily simmered free of the upper shell.

Cut about a pound of this rich meat into small cubes.

Dust with flour. Start the cooking procedures by sautéing a diced onion with a stick of butter in a frypan until soft and golden. Add the meat and, stirring, brown it.

Then pour in a cup of hot water. Add ¼ teaspoon thyme, a very small clove of minced garlic, and salt and freshly ground black pepper to taste. Cover and simmer an hour. Fifteen minutes before done, stir in ¼ cup of sherry. Turtle stewed this way is particularly good when turned over steaming rice.

Turtle Soup

Turtle soup is noteworthy. For about a pound of turtle meat, simmered in a minimum of water until it falls away from the bones which then are removed, take 2 cups of the rich broth.

Blend 2 tablespoons butter and 2 tablespoons flour. Stir into the hot broth. Add ½ teaspoon dry mustard and ¼ teaspoon each of thyme and allspice. Salt and pepper to taste. Simmer, stirring constantly until smooth and thickened. Then stir in the turtle meat which has been cut into small pieces, 2 chopped hard-cooked eggs, and ¼ cup of sherry. Continue simmering another few minutes, whereupon this delicacy will be as carefully composed as a symphony. Serve hot.

Turtle Stroganoff

Cut about 1½ pounds of turtle meat into small, thin strips. Season each with salt and freshly ground black pepper and sprinkle lightly with flour. Melt ½ stick of butter in a frypan and brown the meat in this.

Meanwhile, sauté in another pan with the other ½ stick of butter, ½ pound of sliced fresh mushrooms, and a chopped medium-size onion, cooking them over such low heat that they become soft rather than brown. Add a cup of sour cream and ½ cup of hot water.

Add the turtle, cover, and cook over extremely low heat until the meat is tender. The time for this will vary according to the species. Add a jigger of good sherry and a teaspoon of paprika for that superlative hearty flavor. Season with any necessary salt and freshly ground black pepper. Served with hot toast, rice, or mashed potatoes, this is food that will be savored with an almost sensuous passion.

Chapter Six

Edible Wild Plants:
They're Everywhere

EDIBLE PLANTS GROW wild in every suburban and
rural neighborhood generally within a moment or two
of home. In both small and large cities, vacant lots yield an
amazing harvest. Some of these foods could be produced in
gardens to lend variety to our meals, but when they do appear,
most are pulled up as weeds. Besides it's more fun to seek
them out around fields, old pastures, vacant buildings,
streams, marshes, lakes, ponds, burned-over sections, and
along byways.

Many of these plants you've perhaps already known for
years, although possibly not as good to eat. Others you can
become acquainted with by talking with old-timers who
already use them. Probably the soundest information will
come from wide-ranging source books, such as my *Free for the*

Eating, and *More Free-for-the-Eating Wild Foods*, which describe and illustrate numerous wild edibles in detail. Searching for these wild foods is a marvelously enjoyable outdoor hobby and a delicious way to enliven family meals without any monetary outlay.

Such free foods have always been important in this young country. The Pilgrims derived considerable nourishment during their first desperate winter from groundnuts, which are similar to small potatoes. On the other side of the continent, California's forty-niners, plagued by scurvy because of the scarcity of fresh food in some of the gold camps, were introduced to miner's lettuce by the Indians and the Spanish. Farther north, scurvy grass performed a similar function, both preventing and curing the vitamin-deficiency disease among early frontiersmen.

Wild greens, which should be processed as soon as possible after gathering, can be successfully frozen, but they must be blanched first. This is necessary to halt the enzymatic action which, if not stopped, would change the flavor, color, texture, and even the nutritive values of these delicacies.

To blanch, have a large kettle of water boiling. Place the cleaned greens, not more than two cups for each gallon of fluid, in either a basket or a section of cheesecloth. Lower into the water. Starting counting as soon as boiling is recommenced, scald for two minutes at sea level. Add roughly 10 percent to this total time for each 1,000 feet of higher elevation.

Then cool immediately by plunging the greens into preferably ice water. Drain as well as you can. Get the greens in the form in which you are going to use them, perhaps tearing them into bite sizes. Then dry pack in plastic or laminated containers or bags, leaving one-half inch expansion space at the top. Label, freeze immediately, and store like any other food.

Cooked without defrosting, such wild vegetables can do much to capture for mid-winter enjoyment all the rousing satisfaction and nostalgia of a sunny spring day.

Mountain Sorrel with Eggs

The piquant acid taste of mountain sorrel (*Oxyria*) combines subtly with the delicate flavor of very fresh eggs. Simmer these latter first, completely covered with water, for 10 minutes. Then remove them from the heat and plunge them into cold water. If the shells are cracked slightly before the eggs cool, peeling will be easier.

Slice the eggs in half lengthwise and remove the yolks. Wash and dry some tender young mountain sorrel, chop it into fine bits, and mix your idea of enough with the yolks. Season to taste with salt, freshly ground black pepper, and paprika.

Fill the halved whites with greenish-yellow bulges of the mixture, top each with a bit of butter, sprinkle lightly with Parmesan cheese, and slide beneath a glowing grill until the cheese tans. Serve on a sorrel-bedded platter, garnished with red wedges of well-salted tomato.

Mountain Sorrel Soufflé

The pleasantly lemony flavor of the broad, smooth leaves of mountain sorrel, gathered young, can give a subtle tang to a soufflé. You'll need 2 loosely packed cups of the shredded greens for the following recipe. These should preferably be tender enough not to require any precooking.

Melt 2 tablespoons of butter, slowly stir in 2 tablespoons sifted flour, and cook over low heat for 5 minutes. Heat ½ cup of milk well short of a boil and add it bit by bit to the butter and flour. Seasoning with ½ teaspoon salt and ⅛ teaspoon freshly ground black pepper, stir and cook until very smooth. Mix in the mountain sorrel. Then add 3 beaten egg yolks.

Beat 3 egg whites until stiff. Fold these into the other ingredients, which have been removed from the heat and allowed to cool. Turn immediately into a buttered soufflé dish and bake in a preheated 375° oven for 30 minutes. Have everything at the table ready so you can serve your soufflé immediately.

Mountain Sorrel Soup

In an enamel or stainless steel saucepan, cook a generous ½ pound of chopped mountain sorrel until tender, then drain. You'll want ½ cup of these tangy cooked leaves for enough of this soup to have four anxiously watching the stove. Rinse the pan in which the sorrel was cooked and bring 2 cups of game bird or chicken stock to a simmer, remove from the heat, and smoothly mix in a cup of light cream. Stir that into the stock. Then add the sorrel, a teaspoon of butter, and salt and freshly ground black pepper to taste.

Cook over low heat until seething, stirring constantly. If the liquid becomes too thick for your liking, thin it with cream. Sprinkle sparsely with tarragon and serve hot. Or if you prefer, refrigerate and use as a different chilled soup for an overly warm summer night when perhaps the pale light from a nearly full moon is intensifying the sweltering stillness by hotly etching each motionless leaf and twig.

Braised Scotch Lovage

As Aristotle said, "He who sees things grow from the beginning will have the finest view of them." Scotch lovage is an example. Braised, this wild celery, so rich in vitamins A and C, is singularly tasty with sea food. Gather the young leafy stalks before the Scotch lovage (*Ligusticum*) blossoms, if you can, while they are still tender and succulent.

Cut the stalks into convenient sections, put preferably in cold fish stock, although water can be used instead, and boil them until just tender. Then sauté in butter until lightly tanned. Pour on ½ cup of strong fish stock, stir and cook 3 minutes, and serve at once.

If you enjoy this often, you can vary the taste on occasion by sprinkling a small amount of minced onion, perhaps wild also, over the Scotch lovage while sautéing. But be sparing with the onion or you'll overpower the attractive celery flavor.

Seacoast Angelica Soup

The wild celery known as seacoast angelica (*Angelica*), at its best in late spring and early summer while still tender, is even juicier and tastier than cultivated celery. It is an especially provocative supplement to boiled fish.

For four feasters, simmer a cup of the peeled and chopped hollow green stalks in 2 cups of fish stock until soft. Then press them through a sieve. Add 2 tablespoons of butter that has been smoothly creamed with an equal volume of sifted flour. Pour in the stock and 2 cups of light cream.

Bring to a simmer only, season to taste with salt and freshly ground black pepper, sprinkle with paprika, and serve to your hungry crew. This is invigorating when the long, slanting lines of a warm-weather shower are blowing in gauzy veils through the trees.

Wild Rice

The smoky sweetness of the purple-black, rod-like seeds of wild rice (*Zizania*) blends wonderfully with wild meat, particularly game birds. However, if the wild rice is not washed in cold water before cooking, it will have too much of this smoky flavor. Repeated washing is not necessary, on the other hand, as the slender seeds are not coated.

A basic way of preparing a cup of washed wild rice is to add it slowly to 3 cups of boiling water, seasoned with a teaspoon of salt. Do this gradually so the liquid does not stop bubbling. Then lower the heat to a simmer and cook, uncovered, 30 to 45 minutes or until the particular rice is tender. Shake the kettle now and then to prevent sticking.

Move to a buttered casserole, dot with a tablespoon of chipped butter, cover, and keep warm in a moderate 350° oven for 15 minutes while the seeds become even more fluffy.

You'll generally prefer the flavor unimpaired or, at the most, touched up with a teaspoon of grated onion, but if you're eating a lot of wild rice and sometimes want a change, try adding a teaspoon of finely chopped water cress and ¼ teaspoon basil.

Wild Rice Mold

For enough for four, melt ½ stick of butter in a saucepan and sauté ½ cup of sliced mushrooms. Remove the mushrooms and set aside. Then add to the mushroom liquid in the pan ½ pound washed wild rice, ½ teaspoon salt, and finally 2 cups of boiling stock. Cover and simmer over low heat about 30 minutes, or until a test kernel of rice proves to be tender all the way through.

Then fold in ¼ cup of diced pimento, ¼ cup of chopped water cress, and the reserved mushrooms. Press firmly into a liberally buttered bowl, cover and leave in a warm oven 10 minutes. Uncover the bowl, set a large round platter over this, and then turn both together so you have a colorful wild rice mold in the center of the platter.

Arrange roasted or grilled game birds around this and

serve hot. This is a dish for a day enlivened with the white whirling of snow flurries, when the yellowish light reflected from humped shrubbery all around is like the glare from frozen rivers.

Wild Rice with Livers

Wild rice, one of the favorite foods of Indians and waterfowl on this continent for centuries before even the first Vikings arrived, provides a particularly tasty accompaniment when you are featuring game birds. For enough to serve four, cover a cup of the washed seeds, harvested these days by Wisconsin and Minnesota Indians among others, with 3 cups of boiling water. Stirring occasionally, simmer uncovered about 40 minutes or until the rice is tender and the water absorbed and evaporated.

Keep the rice warm in a double boiler or in the oven while melting a stick of butter in a frypan. Sauté ½ pound of sliced mushrooms in this along with a teaspoon of diced onions, until they are brown and tender. Then add about a cup of game bird livers, or less if you don't have that many, and sauté these until they are well colored. If the rewards from hunting excursions have all been expended, a thawed package of frozen chicken livers can be used instead.

Season to taste with salt and freshly ground black pepper. Then add the wild rice and mix gently. Serve at once preferably with fried or roast fowl. I like this during city autumns when dark strings of ducks are in the air so intriguingly distant that the clamor of a flock may be lost before it is much more than discovered.

Water Cress Sandwiches

Water cress sandwiches are so superb that their creation can be a high art. Variations are, of course, innumerable, but the following may give you a few ideas. Nearly everyone may have a hand at these, for water cress (*Nasturtium*) grows wild over most of North America. Furthermore, it is available the year around except when the waters in which it flourishes are frozen.

Even when you mix water cress with egg, there are a number of ways of going about it. First, provide mealy, appetizing, hard-cooked eggs by keeping them simmering, completely covered with water, for 8 to 10 minutes, depending on size. Do not boil. At the end of this time, remove from the heat and plunge into cold water. Crack the shells slightly as the eggs cool so they will peel more easily.

For one variation, chop 4 hard-cooked eggs. Mix them with 2 tablespoons chopped water cress, ½ teaspoon salt, and ⅛ teaspoon paprika. Spread between buttered bread halves. If you are having a party, cut off the crust and shape the sandwiches into triangles or strips. Or for a robust lunch, eat them "as is" perhaps with whole wheat bread.

For an even smoother filler, you can combine the butter directly with the finely chopped eggs, first letting it soften at room temperature and then mixing and crushing everything to a smooth paste. Season to taste with salt, grated onion, chopped chives, mustard, or with what you will. Then spread on one slice of bread. Top liberally with sprigs of water cress and cover with a second slice.

Cream cheese and bacon can also come into the act. To go with a small package of the former, you'll need ½ cup of diced, cooked bacon. Start this in a cold frypan and cook over low heat, tilting the pan so the grease will flow away from the tanning, drying bits. Beat cheese, bacon, ⅛ teaspoon salt, ⅛ teaspoon paprika, and ¾ cup of chopped water cress to a paste along with 2 tablespoons of light cream. This spread is effective on any kind of bread or toast, but for something special try it sometime on thin slices of rye.

Or if your hunger precludes all such preparations, just butter both slices of bread plentifully so the cress does not make the sandwich limp and soggy. Fill liberally with chopped water cress sprinkled with lemon juice.

Water Cress Salad

Because its use can be traced beyond the Romans and Greeks to the early Persians, water cress has been called the most ancient of wild green vegetables. Even though Xerxes, King of Persia nearly 500 years before the birth of Christ, knew nothing of its teeming minerals and vitamins, he recommended the crisp edible for maintaining the health of his armies.

To enjoy water cress at its best, eat it relatively unadorned. The following simple salad, for example, has been a universal favorite whenever we've served it. Freshly gathered water cress is best. If you're going to keep the green for several days, wash it carefully in cold water, dry it, and store it until just before use in a covered container in the refrigerator.

For the salad, place enough of the crisp sprigs for four in a salad bowl. Sprinkle with ½ teaspoon salt, ½ teaspoon freshly ground black pepper, ⅛ teaspoon paprika, and 3 tablespoons olive oil. Toss lightly just before serving.

Hot Weather Salad

One of the most refreshing water cress salads is the easiest to prepare. Simply fill a bowl with sprigs of water cress, well washed in cold water and then thoroughly dried. Slice oranges over them. Cover with dressing made by dissolving ½ teaspoon of salt in ¼ cup of lemon juice, stirring in ¼ teaspoon of freshly ground black pepper, and then whipping in ¾ cup of olive oil. Toss at the table.

Water Cress with Eggs

You'll find this a welcome way to prepare scrambled eggs. For each serving, mix 3 eggs and 3 tablespoons cold water with salt and freshly ground black pepper to taste. Heat a tablespoon of butter in a frypan just hot enough to bounce a drop of water. Pour in the egg mixture and reduce the heat.

When the eggs have commenced to harden, start beating them continuously with a fork. Remove them while they are still very soft and creamy. Place them in a moderate 325° oven with the door ajar to finish cooking even more slowly.

Heat a tablespoon of your best wine vinegar until about half of it has evaporated. Then pour it separately over the eggs, followed by a tablespoon of well-colored butter in which you have browned 2 tablespoons of finely chopped water cress. Such a repast will send a pleasant languor spreading over everyone.

Fried Water Cress

To complete that epicurean enjoyment of freshly caught fish or shellfish, garnish them with fried water cress. Just toss the individual sprigs into hot oil for scarcely a minute. Drain briefly on absorbent paper. This really touches up those mouthfuls of hot steaming trout, especially when served with a delicate white wine.

Winter Cress Soup

The somewhat radish-like savor of winter cress (*Barbarea*)— whose smooth, dark green leaves often push up during mild winter weather where the ground is bare of snow—goes well in the following cream soup which you can start in your electric blender. However, taste the winter cress first. The leaves of this widespread member of the mustard family become overly bitter with age, whereupon you may prefer to parboil them first.

For enough savory soup for four, combine 3 cups of light cream, 3 tablespoons of butter, a teaspoon of salt, ⅛ teaspoon paprika, and a tightly packed cup of chopped winter cress in the blender. Run until smoothly mixed. Then, stirring, simmer over low heat for 5 minutes. That's all. Serve hot.

This one really rolls back those seasons, as outside the deciduous trees still have a bare and shelterless aspect, with only the evergreens, which keep up their sap all winter, having a feeling of warmth about them.

Fireweed and Eggs

The asparagus-like flavor of young fireweed stalks (*Epilobium*), whose magenta flower spikes later enhance thousands of square miles of scorched wilderness from Mexico to Greenland and the Aleutians, combines delicately with that of fresh eggs. For enough to serve two hungry vacationers, you'll want 2 cups of these, cut into 1-inch sections. Use only the tenderest portions, gathered well before the silken flight of fireweed floss covers the countryside.

Heat 2 tablespoons of butter and 2 tablespoons of olive oil in a heavy frypan until they start to tan. Add the fireweed and stir for 3 minutes. Then pour in a cup of boiling water, cover, and simmer for about 3 more minutes or until a fork can be easily inserted in the larger of the segments. Do not let the green become mushy, however.

Have 6 fresh, well-beaten eggs seasoned with salt and freshly ground black pepper to taste and mixed with ½ cup of newly grated Parmesan cheese and ½ cup of fine, dry, white bread crumbs. Stir into the bubbling mixture in the frypan. Lower the heat. Continue mixing gently for several minutes until the eggs are creamy.

Sprinkle with 2 tablespoons of chopped water cress. Strew with vitamin-teeming paprika. Serve immediately on warm plates, along with hot garlic toast yellow with butter.

Nettle Balls

In the springtime, when young nettles are shooting up like green fire, you can accompany your freshly caught fish with a toothsome, different vegetable dish. For enough to satiate four hungry anglers, you'll need 2 cups of these cooked, chopped, single-stemmed greens, most handily gathered with leather gloves and a sharp knife. As soon as the salted water has reached the bubbling stage and the dark green nettles have been dropped in, they'll be sufficiently tender almost immediately and will have lost all stinging qualities.

Chop the cooked nettles and mix them with 2 table-spoons apiece of either chopped chives or grated onion, butter, and freshly grated Parmesan cheese. Work in a cup of fine, dry, white bread crumbs, seasoned with ⅛ teaspoon salt, and a coloring of freshly ground black pepper. Allow to stand 15 minutes until the crumbs absorb some of the moisture.

Then form into balls. Roll each of these in additional bread crumbs, dip in egg that has been briefly beaten with ⅓ cup cold water, and roll once more in the crumbs. Fry about

3 minutes, until tan and tempting in deep fat. Have everything timed so you can serve these sizzling hot.

Wild Onion Sauce

Wild onions (*Allium*), seasoning mainstay of the American Indians who gathered them in nearly all the States and in southern Canada, can do much to turn a venison steak into a gourmet's delight.

For enough of this special steak sauce for four, melt ½ stick of butter in a small, heavy frypan. As soon as the butter begins to color, add 1½ cups of thinly sliced wild onions. Lowering the heat, keep turning these so they'll tan evenly. While they are still slightly crisp, pour in ¼ cup of good sherry. Bring everything to a simmer, stir thoroughly and tip immediately over the still noisy meat.

Cocktail Sandwiches

These will really have your guests sampling and talking and devouring. The basic ingredients you'll need are water cress and wild onions. Slice the latter as thin as possible.

An electric blender will ease the preparation of the water cress dressing, although you also can blend this by hand. The fact that you'll only have to chop ¼ cup of cress makes it not too difficult.

If you are using a blender, commence by blending the washed and dried water cress, along with 2 tablespoons of lemon juice, until you have a bright green mass. Add to this ¼ cup olive oil, a whole egg, ½ teaspoon salt, ½ teaspoon sugar, ½ teaspoon dry mustard, and ¼ teaspoon freshly ground black pepper. Mix everything well.

Now start pouring in ¾ cup of olive oil, adding only a small amount at a time and running the blender at high speed for about 5 seconds at each stage or until all the oil has been intermingled with the egg and water cress mixture. If you make this beforehand, store it in a covered container in the refrigerator.

For the appetizers, cut thin slices of some finely textured bread. Divide these into bite-size triangles. Spread each with the green mayonnaise. Top half the triangles with a single layer of thinly sliced wild onion. Cover with the other triangles to make sandwiches.

Spread the remaining dressing on a sheet of wax paper and, holding each sandwich lightly by its center, immerse each edge in the mayonnaise. Then touch to a small heap of finely chopped water cress. Chill in the refrigerator before serving.

Wild Onion Soup

Game bird or venison stock provides a tasty basis for this queen of the wild soups. You'll need a quart if you are serving four.

Start by melting ½ stick of butter in the bottom of a saucepan. Brown a cup of thinly sliced wild onions in this.

Then sprinkle with a tablespoon of sifted flour and stir over moderate heat for 5 more minutes. Add the stock, preferably hot, and cook at no more than a simmer until the onion is extremely tender.

In the meantime, cut 4 slices of preferably sourdough bread as thinly as you can. Cover liberally with freshly grated Parmesan cheese and melt this quickly under the broiler. Tip the soup into a warm tureen, top with the toast, and serve without delay. The aroma will be so piquant and tantalizing that no one will be able to wait.

Wild Onions and Toast

There are numerous North American species of wild onions belonging to the pleasantly odiferous *Allium* family, but the ones I've gathered for years along the Peace River in northwestern Canada are so mild that they boil up deliciously in a small amount of water. However, if the variety near your home is strongly flavored, you may prefer to parboil them first and to discard the first water. However, at the end drop the clean and peeled onions into rapidly boiling salted water and cook briskly until a sharp fork can be easily inserted and withdrawn.

Drain well and serve on hot toast, well covered with melted butter that has been diluted with a little of the liquid in which the onions were boiled. If the onions are particularly sweet, you also may wish to add a small quantity of dry sherry to the melted butter.

Wild Onions and Bear

It's probably just as well that more individuals haven't sat down to this paragon of repasts, for if they had, the amiable black bear probably wouldn't be making so much of a comeback in many sections of the continent. You can bake it in the oven at the same time you're cooking that roast haunch.

One feature of this recipe is that it can be adapted to any number of eaters. Just set alternate layers of wild onions and apple rings in a well-buttered casserole. Moisten with broth made by simmering a few odds and ends of bear meat in lightly salted water for several hours. Cover with dry white bread crumbs, seasoned to taste with salt and freshly ground black pepper. Dot with butter and bake an hour in a moderate 325° oven, just the right temperature for that roasting bruin.

Wild Leeks and Eggs

The fragrant wild leek (*Allium*), familiar in our eastern woodlands, was a standby of Indian women for everything from soups and salads to stews. To serve four, try chopping enough of the bulbs and green tops to fill a cup. Sauté in 3 tablespoons of bacon fat until tender.

In the meantime, beat 8 eggs with a teaspoon of salt and ¼ teaspoon of freshly ground black pepper until everything is well mixed. Stir in 4 tablespoons of sherry and 2 tablespoons light cream. Pour over the wild leeks and reduce the heat. When the eggs have started to set, begin stirring them constantly with a fork. If removed from the pan while still creamy, this will really please the palate.

Mustard with Scrambled Eggs

Legend has it that when the Padres were lengthening their notable Mission Trail through California, they planted mustard seed along the route. By the time they returned, the way was conspicuously marked with this hardy annual which now flourishes wild in nearly every part of the temperate zone.

Today young tender mustard leaves are more often used to add vitamins and character to scrambled eggs. For enough for two, lightly beat 4 eggs and 4 tablespoons light cream with ¼ teaspoon of salt and a dash of freshly ground black pepper. Add a cup of shredded mustard (*Brassica*) leaves.

Heat 2 tablespoons of butter in a frypan, just hot enough to make a few drops of water hiss. Pour in the mustard and egg mixture and cook slowly, stirring occasionally. Remove when almost set, but still moist, and see if you don't agree that this has a place in the most complex and refined cuisine.

Cream of Mustard Soup

The tender young leaves of wild mustard, whose edible yellow flowers turn fields all over the world into golden expanses, cook down considerably when simmered in salted water, and you'll need to end up with 2 cupfuls for this recipe. Chop these cooked greens and press them through a sieve.

You may choose now to turn to a double boiler, as this soup should not boil. Melt 3 tablespoons butter, blend in a tablespoon of flour, and add a quart of milk. When this has heated, stir in the mustard and ½ cup of heavy cream. Season to taste with salt and freshly ground black pepper. Let this heat for 10 minutes. Then serve piping hot.

Freshly made croutons go well with this soup, although I prefer toasted cheese sandwiches fashioned from thin slices of dark bread.

Mustard Molds

The slightly peppery young leaves of wild mustard can be combined with eggs to make tasty hot molds, excellent with fish. For sufficient to serve four, you'll need to cook up enough of the greens in simmering salted water to fill 1½ cups. Chop the verdant mass into fine bits and put these through a sieve. Then press out as much of the moisture as you can.

Mix this mustard puree with ½ stick melted butter, 3 beaten eggs, a cup of warmed light cream, a tablespoon of grated onion, and ½ teaspoon salt. Distribute among 4 well-buttered custard cups or other containers, placing these in a shallow pan whose bottom is filled with water.

Bake in a preheated moderate 375° oven for 35 minutes or until the molds are set. First loosening the edges with a knife, turn each receptacle upside down over a warm platter and tap the mold loose. Garnish with sliced, hard-cooked egg, sprinkle with paprika, and serve while still steaming. These are as delightful to the eyes as to the taste buds.

Ham and Mustard Green Soup

If you're wondering how to use the rest of that ham and wild mustard which is flourishing about, here's a piquant solution that four diners will sip with gusto. You'll need about ⅓ pound of diced ham and 4 loosely packed cups of young mustard leaves, torn into bite-size pieces.

Cover the ham with a quart of water, add 2 teaspoons soy sauce and a teaspoon powdered ginger, bring to a bubble, and allow to cook 10 minutes. Then add the greens and simmer, uncovered, only until these are sufficiently tender. Season to taste with salt and serve.

Lamb's-Quarters Salad

Even when the majority of lamb's-quarters' (*Chenopodium*) pale green leaves with their mealy-appearing undersides become too tough to eat raw, you can still enjoy a salad with this tastiest of the wild spinach family. Pick enough of the greens to simmer in salted water into 2 cupfuls.

For the dressing, combine 4 tablespoons olive oil, a tablespoon fresh lemon juice, 2 teaspoons grated onion, 1 teaspoon salt, ¼ teaspoon dry mustard, and ⅛ teaspoon freshly ground black pepper. Mix this thoroughly with the cooked greens and chill.

Even late in the summer, you can strip a quantity of small tender leaves from this wild vegetable, also widely known as pigweed and goosefoot. Do this just before your meal, providing 4 verdant layers on which to heap the individual servings of the salad. And, particularly if it's hot weather, see what the family's idea is for vegetables the rest of the week.

Creamed Dandelion Greens

The familiar dandelion (*Taraxacum*), all too well known because of the way it dots many a lawn, is among the best of the wild greens. Four cups of the washed and very thoroughly dried young leaves, with a few buds included for flavor and appearance, will make a salad for as many feasters. Put these into a bowl and sprinkle them with 1½ teaspoons salt. Pour a cup of sour cream over the top and color this with ¼ teaspoon of freshly ground black pepper and ⅛ teaspoon of paprika.

Add a tablespoon of chopped chives if the greens are very young. If they are older, just short of being tough, their own singular flavor will be sufficient. Toss at the table.

Dandelion Soup

Succulent young dandelion leaves continue to be numbered among the very first wild edibles I gather while trout fishing in the early spring, especially because they combine so well with fish stock when you want to manufacture a zestful soup.

You can come by this later in the season, too, just by cooking the dandelions longer.

The way to start enough for four is by sautéing a small grated onion with 2 tablespoons of butter in a saucepan until tender. Then pour in 2 cups of fish stock. Bring to a bubble. Stir in 4 cups of torn dandelion greens, including as many buds as reasonable. Simmer over low heat until the greens are wilted and tender, seasoning to taste with salt and freshly ground black pepper.

While this cooking is continuing, beat together 2 egg yolks and ½ cup heavy cream. Mix this into the soup and stir over low heat, well short of the boiling point, until the mixture thickens. Add any necessary salt and pepper, touch up with paprika, and serve.

Cattail Hotcakes

When the sausage-like flower spike of the widely known cattail (*Typhaeeae*) becomes golden with thick yellow pollen, you can enjoy some unusual pancakes. First, collect a cup of pollen by rubbing or shaking it into a container or onto a cloth. Mix it with a cup of flour. Then sift together pollen, flour, 2 tablespoons baking powder, 2 tablespoons sugar, and ½ teaspoon salt.

Beat 2 eggs and stir them, along with 2 tablespoons melted butter, into 1⅓ cups milk. Then rapidly mix the batter. Pour immediately in cakes the size of saucers onto a sparingly greased griddle, short of being smoking hot. Turn each hotcake only once, when the flapjack begins showing tiny bubbles. The second side takes only about half as long to cook.

Serve steaming hot with butter and sugar, with maple syrup, or with what you will. They'll be as outstandingly novel as they are eye-catching.

Wilted Shepherd's-Purse

Thriving so close to the ground and in such accessible places, shepherd's-purse (*Capsella*) is apt to pick up a lot of grit and dust, so it is best to gather the leaves young and then to wash them well.

To steam enough for four people, melt 4 tablespoons of butter in a heavy frypan over high heat. Stir in 6 loosely filled cups of greens, along with 6 tablespoons of water. Cover, except when stirring periodically, and cook for several minutes until the leaves are wilted. Salt, pepper, and serve.

Plantain with Vinegar Sauce

This is geared to enough tender, young plantain (*Plantago*) leaves for four. Tear these into bite-size pieces in a salad bowl.

Starting with a cold frypan, fry 8 slices of bacon until crisp. Then remove them from the pan, drain on absorbent paper, and crumble.

Sauté a tablespoon of chopped onion in the hot fat. As soon as the bits are brown, add ½ cup vinegar, a tablespoon sugar, a teaspoon salt, and ⅛ teaspoon freshly ground black pepper, all mixed with a beaten egg. Stirring, heat until thick and bubbly. Then pour over the greens, stirring everything together thoroughly.

Sprinkle the bacon over the top, garnish with a sliced, hard-cooked egg, sprinkle with paprika, and serve.

Spicy Plantain Roast

For one of those warm, lazy days plantain, deliciously and universally distributed throughout the world, can be used to make a one-dish meal. You'll need 2 cups of cooked and drained young plantain leaves.

Mix these with a large can of tomatoes, a cup of dry white bread crumbs, ½ cup of grated Cheddar cheese, a medium-size chopped onion, and 2 teaspoons Worcestershire sauce. Spread everything out in a well-buttered pan or casserole, sprinkle with paprika, and lay 8 slices of bacon on top. Bake in a moderate 350° oven for an hour. That's all. As has been noted, laziness in doing things can sometimes be a great virtue.

Purslane Salad

Add a halved clove of garlic to ½ cup of olive oil and allow to stand all morning or afternoon. Then remove the garlic. With everything ready to go, tear enough purslane (*Portulaca*) into bite-size pieces in a salad bowl.

Stir ¼ teaspoon salt, ⅛ teaspoon freshly ground black

pepper, and ⅛ teaspoon dry mustard into the oil. Then add ½ cup of crumbled blue cheese.

Pour over the delicately acid greens and toss lightly. Add the juice of a fresh lemon and a beaten whole raw egg. Toss again. Correct the salt and pepper if necessary. Finally, toss in ½ cup of fresh croutons, lightly browned in a tablespoon of olive oil.

All this will really enhance the fresh and different flavor of this long-popular edible, a favorite of Henry Thoreau, who once observed, "It would be some advantage to lead a primitive life, although in the midst of civilization, if only to learn what are the necessaries."

Wild Lettuce Salad

Variety is the password to salad success, and a sure way to avoid monotony lies in learning to identify and use the numerous tender, young, edible wild greens. The widely distributed wild lettuce (*Lactuca*) is an example. Some hot spring day tear a quantity of the leaves (and the tender stems if you wish) into bite sizes. Wash, dry, and chill.

Rub a cut clove of garlic with the tip of a spoon against the inside of a bowl until the herb disappears. Fill the bowl with as much wild lettuce as you are going to need. Top with salt, freshly ground black pepper, and the very thin slices of some sweet oranges that have been cooled in the refrigerator.

Then sprinkle crumbled crisp bacon over everything, a thin slice per serving being a good proportion. It's sound practice, if you have the time, to start broiling this bacon about 6 inches from the heat ½ hour ahead of time. When most of the fat has been cooked out of the pieces, lay them well apart on paper toweling in the warm oven until the moment comes to use them.

Lamb's Lettuce Salad

Lamb's lettuce (*Valerianella*) makes an especially pleasant salad, particularly if about ¼ as much water cress is added to touch up its delicate flavor. Wash the tender young leaves well, afterwards drying them in a towel. Otherwise, the dressing will slip off and form a pool in the bottom of the salad bowl.

Tear, don't cut, these greens into bite-size segments and toss them lightly with enough olive oil and vinegar, mixed 4 parts to 1, to coat them. Arrange contrasting red tomato slices for trim. These tomatoes tend to become too watery if tossed with the greens. Serve without delay.

Miner's Lettuce Au Gratin

Miner's lettuce (*Montia*), so called when it was adopted by California's stampeding forty-niners after the lack of fresh food had brought the vitamin-deficiency disease of scurvy to some of the gold camps, combines subtly with cheese. For four healthy appetites, you'll need 4 loosely packed cups of the tender young leaves of this easily identified green, also known as Indian lettuce and Spanish lettuce and in Europe as winter purslane.

For the necessary sauce, melt 2 tablespoons of butter in a frypan over moderate heat. Sauté a tablespoon of chopped onion slightly, not letting either it or the butter brown. Then stir in 2 tablespoons of flour. Once this is smoothly blended, slowly add a cup of warm milk, stirring constantly. Bring everything to a bubble, seasoning to taste with salt and freshly ground black pepper. Simmer for 5 minutes.

Place alternate layers of miner's lettuce and sauce in a casserole, sprinkle each with freshly grated cheese and fine white bread crumbs. Chip 2 tablespoons of butter over the top and brown in a moderate 350° oven. This is the finest spring tonic that anyone could want.

Cream of Wild Lettuce Soup

Prickly lettuce (*Lactuca*), the familiar coast-to-coast delicacy from which some botanists think our cultivated lettuce was developed, can be the main ingredient in an enjoyable cream of wild lettuce soup. Begin by sautéing a diced, medium-size onion in 2 tablespoons of butter over low heat. When it is soft but before it has begun to brown, add a chopped clove of garlic and 4 loosely packed cups of shredded, tender, young prickly lettuce leaves. Stirring, cook for 3 minutes.

Then pour in a cup of hot stock made from whatever game is to provide the main course, or flavor the cup of water with a bouillon cube. After this has simmered for 12 minutes, add a cup of rich milk and warm just short of a boil.

In the meantime, beat an egg yolk with ½ cup of light cream, stir in an equal portion of the soup, and then pour bit by bit into the whole. As soon as everything reaches a bubble, crown with paprika, and serve. This will delight the most select group of sophisticated epicures.

Horseradish Soup

In the springtime the tender young leaves of this basis of the well-known condiment, made by mixing the grated roots with a little vinegar, will provide an estimable soup with which to inaugurate a fish dinner. Begin with a quart of fish stock, prepared by boiling the heads, tails, bones, and fins in the water, then straining this. Chop the horseradish (*Armoracia*) leaves and simmer 2 cups of them in the stock for 15 minutes.

Dice ½ pound of bacon. Starting it in a cold frypan and pouring off the grease before any large amount accumulates, sauté it along with a diced, medium-size onion until both are tan. Add to the soup, salt and pepper to taste, and sprinkle with nutmeg. Simmer 20 minutes. Then stir in a cup of light cream, warm a minute longer, and serve, with croutons if you wish. This soup has a rousing authority to it, particularly if the bacon is redolent with wood smoke.

Horseradish Sauce

The familiar horseradish, whose young stalks and leaves cook up into tasty greens, can really satisfy those who like to add character to their steaks, chops, and roasts. The part of the perennial used for this is the long whitish root. For a sauce that will really start those taste buds thrilling, grate 3 tablespoons of the freshly dug root. Combine with ⅛ teaspoon salt and a similar volume of paprika. Mix with ½ stick of soft butter.

Horseradish Dip

Wild horseradish, particularly abundant in the northeastern United States and southern Canada, can also be turned into a dip that will enliven any cocktail party. One we like is commenced by mashing and beating 3 tablespoons of freshly grated horseradish with 2 small packages of cream cheese and enough sour cream to give you the consistency you want. Season to taste with salt and freshly ground black pepper, and relegate to the refrigerator to take on flavor.

Before using this, scatter 2 tablespoons of finely chopped water cress over it and, for added color and vitamins, strew with paprika. For a taste change on occasion, you may also care to sprinkle it with a tablespoon of chopped chives. Either way, this dip is especially effective with potato chips and crisp little crackers.

Wild Mint Sauce

Wild mints (*Mentha*), quickly identified by their square stems, opposite leaves, and familiar aroma, grow everywhere. Mint sauce, with an agreeableness all its own, brings out the flavor of venison and other wild meats, especially the king of them all, mountain sheep.

I like mine made by mashing a cup of chopped fresh mint into 2 tablespoons sugar and ¼ teaspoon salt. Mix this with ¾ cup of white vinegar and ¼ cup of freshly squeezed lemon juice. If you concoct this about lunch time and then set it resolutely aside to assume its own mellowness, it will be ready for dinner.

Candied Mint Leaves

Candied mint leaves, perhaps prepared as gifts for friends, provide a refreshing garnish for fruit salads, dessert, and of course iced tea. They also are appealing tidbits by themselves.

Just dip the fresh clean leaves in unbeaten egg white. Then press them into confectioner's sugar. Spread apart on wax paper, lightly dusted with more of the sugar, and relegate to the refrigerator until hard. These candied leaves can then be packed between layers of wax paper in tightly closed containers.

Green Amaranth Soufflé

Green amaranth (*Amaranthus*), whose seeds can later be ground into meal for use in cereals and breadstuffs, makes a delicate, wonderful vegetable when young. Melt 3 tablespoons of butter in a frypan over low heat. Gradually stir in 2 tablespoons of flour and then, bit by bit, ½ cup of warm milk. Season with ½ teaspoon salt and ⅛ teaspoon freshly ground black pepper. Cook until smooth and thick.

Beat the yolks of 4 eggs in a bowl. Gradually stir in the hot sauce, then 2 cups of tender, young, shredded green amaranth leaves. Allow everything to cool. Then fold in the stiffly beaten whites of the 4 eggs, turn into a buttered soufflé dish, and bake in a moderate 375° oven for half an hour or until firm. This is as uniquely enjoyable as it is nourishing.

Sautéed Jerusalem Artichokes

The distinctively flavored, nonstarchy tubers of the Jerusalem artichoke (*Helianthus*), a native wild sunflower formerly cultivated by the Indians, are crisply sweet when sautéed. Just slice them, either scraped or left unpeeled, and sauté them in butter in a large heavy frypan for about 8 minutes, or until bronzed and tender, turning them several times.

If you so enjoy these knobby tubers often, you may care to vary this process on occasion. For a pound of Jerusalem artichokes which will serve 4, heat ½ stick of butter and ¼ cup of salad oil in the skillet. Sauté 2 tablespoons chopped chives until well colored.

Then add the sliced tubers, season with ½ teaspoon salt and ⅛ teaspoon freshly ground black pepper, and sauté, stirring occasionally, for 5 minutes. Pour in ¼ cup of good cider vinegar, bring to a bubble, and simmer for 5 minutes longer. Serve hot. This will really add the crowning touch to a fall evening alive with crickets singing outside in the grass.

Jerusalem Artichoke Salad

Jerusalem artichokes, which have about the same texture as that of cabbage stalks and taste something like a combination of particularly delicate radishes and new potatoes, make fine salad. Just dice enough of the long vegetables for four. Place in a wooden salad bowl, well rubbed with garlic.

Mix ½ cup olive oil, ¼ cup cider vinegar, a tablespoon chopped chives, a teaspoon sugar, ½ teaspoon salt, and ⅛ teaspoon freshly ground black pepper. Toss this with the salad and let everything stand at room temperature for several hours to take on flavor. Toss again at the table and serve. Never was there a salad more fragile, more luxurious, more ingenious.

Jerusalem Artichoke Soup

Jerusalem artichokes are another of the wild vegetables so easily digestible that they are recommended for invalid diets. Wash and scrape about a pound of these wholesome tubers.

As soon as each is ready, drop it into a cup apiece of milk and water to prevent its darkening in the air. Simmer over low heat until soft.

Then press the vegetables through a sieve. Return them to the saucepan, along with the milk and water, ½ cup of light cream, a tablespoon of butter, and salt to taste. Stir until everything begins bubbling, and then simmer for 5 minutes before serving.

Chickweed Omelet

For four diners who never believed the abundantly distributed common chickweed (*Stellaria*) was good to eat, chop 2 cups of the tender top stems and leaves. Sauté these until soft in 2 tablespoons of olive oil in a frypan over low heat. Then sprinkle in ½ teaspoon salt and ⅛ teaspoon freshly ground black pepper. Simmer for 10 minutes. Stir in ¼ cup of freshly grated Parmesan cheese and simmer 5 minutes more.

In the meantime, break 9 eggs into a bowl, add 3 tablespoons cold water, ½ teaspoon salt, and ⅛ teaspoon freshly ground black pepper, and beat with a fork until the eggs are broken up but not whipped.

In a separate skillet, heat 3 tablespoons of butter until it begins to brown. Pour in the eggs. Keep shaking and slanting the pan slightly while cooking so as to keep the omelet from sticking. As soon as the bottom of the omelet starts to harden, slip a thin spatula or knife well under the edges and lift the middle so uncooked egg can flow beneath it. This liquid egg will repair any resulting breaks and tears.

As soon as the eggs no longer flow freely, but the top still looks moist and creamy, spread the hot chickweed over half of the omelet. Fold the remaining half over this by tilting the pan sideways with one hand and then lifting the uppermost section over the middle. Now shake, tilt, and slide the folded omelet onto a hot platter. Serve immediately so as not to lose any of the rich, golden savoriness.

Sunflower Seed Soup

Although sunflower seeds are now sold at many a counter, the Indians, according to Lewis and Clark's Journal of 1805, early made "great use of the seed of this plant for bread, or in thickening their soup."

If you'd like to try this soup with the seeds of one of the wild sunflowers (*Helianthus*) which still grow wild over much of the Americas, shell 1½ cups of them for enough soup for four. Place them in a saucepan along with 4 cups of game bird or chicken stock, 2 tablespoons chopped chives, and salt to taste. Simmer, stirring occasionally, for 40 minutes. Serve while flavors and aromas you've never dreamed of are still steaming from it.

Candied Sweet Flag

Candied sweet flag (*Acorus calamus*), which I've bought on a number of occasions along the downtown streets of my native

Boston, has somewhat the same aromatic pungency of the now often difficult-to-obtain candied ginger.

To make your own, cut either the fleshy rootstocks or the tender base of the stalks into very thin slices. Parboil the first especially in 1 or even 2 changes of water to remove some of the bitterness. Then simmer, stirring frequently, in a syrup composed proportionately of a cup of sugar to ½ cup of water until almost all of the sugar has been absorbed.

Groundnut Omelet

Groundnuts (*Apios*), which helped Swedish settlers through breadless days on the Delaware during Colonial times, still cook up into mighty special food. If you are serving two, for instance, thinly slice 2 cups of them, leaving them unpeeled. Sauté them in 3 tablespoons olive oil until well colored. Add ½ cup of diced onion and cook this until it is limp. Add ½ cup chopped water cress and mix thoroughly. Salt and pepper to taste.

Then break 4 eggs into a bowl. Add a tablespoon of water, ¼ teaspoon salt, and just a dash of freshly ground black pepper. Beat vigorously with a fork until the yolks and whites are blended. Pour this over the other ingredients. Cook until the eggs no longer run freely when the pan is slanted, but the moistly inviting top still looks creamy.

Sea Moss Blancmange

The seaweed called Irish moss (*Chondrus*), common along the Atlantic shores of Canada and the United States where it can be gathered at low tide, cooks up into a delicate blancmange which is so digestible that many drug stores stock it for invalid diets. You can harvest this moss at any season, wash it well in fresh water, and then dry it for future use. Spread out in the sun, it bleaches a pearly white.

When ready to cook, soak ½ cup of this iodine-rich marine alga, also called carrageen moss, for 20 minutes in enough cold water to cover it. Then drain and pick out any discolored bits. Add what is left to a quart of milk in the top of a double boiler. Cook over boiling water for 30 minutes. Then strain the milk.

Stir ¼ cup sugar, a teaspoon vanilla, and ¼ teaspoon salt into the strained milk. Turn into cups or molds that have been immersed in cold water, chill in the refrigerator until firm, and then serve with cream and sugar. A topping of wild strawberries really sets these off.

Fiddleheads

A supper of young fiddleheads (*Pteridium*) on hot buttered toast sets just right for individuals who don't feel like eating much. When served this way, the little wild vegetables retain more of their delicate flavor when steamed.

After they have been cleaned and washed, drop them into

2 tablespoons of boiling water in the top of a double boiler. Cover the utensil, place over boiling water, and cook for a half-hour. The best way to continue preserving the distinctive flavor is just to salt each serving lightly to individual taste, then top it with a liberal chunk of butter.

Fiddlehead Salad

Fiddleheads always bring back the faint scent of spring which comes in part from the first flowers and partly from the damp bark of the trees and shrubs. The shrill, piping cries of the spring peepers, the oldest sound on earth, is like the almost forgotten jingle of sleigh bells, although no longer is there any sharpness of winter in the breeze. A faraway whiff of wood smoke goes with it.

Especially in these parts of the continent where the tightly curled tips of the edible ferns are among the first greens of the year, fiddlehead salad can be a gourmet treat. Cook the cleaned fiddleheads in a small amount of salted water as before.

Then marinate them for several hours in the refrigerator with an equal volume of sliced onions. These onions should be mixed half and half with dressing made proportionately by dissolving ½ teaspoon salt in ¼ cup tarragon vinegar, stirring in ¼ teaspoon freshly ground black pepper, and whipping with ¾ cup olive oil.

Chapter Seven

Wild Fruit:
Free for the Picking

DELICIOUS WILD FRUITS grow everywhere. It's difficult to journey across any part of the United States, from the scorching deserts to where the ice pack glitters off northern Alaska, that does not regularly yield wholesome and usually delectable crops.

No tame cherry has yet been developed that has the savor of the plump ripe rum cherry, so popular during early New England days. The wild strawberries perfuming the air from the Arctic Circle to Florida and California are far sweeter than domestic varieties. As for wild cranberries, still regarded by many as the most important berry of the north country, the untamed species have the most flavor and color.

Where can you find a domestic fruit like the highbush cranberry (no relation), especially during the frosty seasons when the sweetish sour berries will melt on your tongue like sherbet? Wild mulberries, one of the favorite foods of songbirds and small game, make pies you have to eat to believe. When it comes to the wild elderberry, you can use the flowers in your cooking, feast on the berries, and make flutes Indian fashion from the limbs. It still takes wild blueberries, often so thick that they can be gathered by the bushel just by shaking them onto outspread sheets, to rejuvenate thousands of acres of fire-blackened woodlands.

Freshly picked and carefully handled blackberries, elderberries, strawberries, currants, raspberries, gooseberries, blueberries, mulberries, highbush cranberries, and salmonberries retain their refreshing flavor and rich color for a long time when frozen by the dry pack method. Just pick them over and stem them. Spread on trays until frozen. Then pour like marbles into rigid containers or plastic bags and store. When these are served, a few remaining ice crystals will enhance both their savor and shape.

Rum cherries, which may be pitted if storage space is a problem, may well be covered with a cooled syrup made by dissolving three cups of sugar in every quart of water, along with one-half teaspoon of ascorbic acid to prevent further darkening.

Persimmons should be peeled, then packed in a syrup made by dissolving two cups of sugar in each quart of water. A tablespoon of fresh lemon juice should then be added to every five cups of syrup.

Blackberry Pie

Like many of the other members of the vast rose family, blackberries (*Rubus*) make superb pies. Mix 2 tablespoons cornstarch, a cup sugar, and ⅛ teaspoon salt. Blend gradually with ½ cup cold water. Bring this slowly to a simmer and, stirring, cook a minute. Combine with 3 cups wild blackberries, turn into an uncooked pie shell, cover liberally with chips of butter, and top with a second layer of pastry.

Bake in a preheated hot 450° oven for 10 minutes. Then reduce the heat to a moderate 350° and bake 30 minutes longer or until done.

A good crust for this and for other 9-inch, double-crust wild berry pies can be made by carefully combining ⅓ cup of good shortening with 2 cups all-purpose flour sifted with 1 teaspoon salt until what you reach is about the same consistency as corn meal.

Then add another ⅓ cup shortening and blend until the flour is completely absorbed and you have a consistency like that of large peas. Incidentally, by far the best shortening both for flavor and for texture that we have ever found for pies is rendered bear fat, described in the chapter on big game.

Add by teaspoonfuls 5 to 6 tablespoons cold water, tossing lightly with a fork until the mixture is barely dampened. Gather into a ball in waxed paper, then chill. Cut this in half. Roll each half out, on a plastic or other surface well dusted with the same type of flour, until it is about ⅛ inch thick.

Invert the pie dish or preferably, the well-browned pie tin

on the dough. Allow ½-inch margin when you trim. In those cases when you want a precooked shell, prick the shell with tines of a fork, then bake in a hot 450° oven until tan, about 15 minutes.

Devoured hot during a snowstorm, with the vague moving whiteness becoming gray as darkness approaches, such blackberry pie really brings back the languid days of summer.

Cold Blackberry Soup

When the weather is sweltering and the wild blackberries ripen, the following cold soup can be as cheering as hot buttered rum in a blizzard. For enough to serve four, 2 cups of the fresh fruit will suffice. Press the berries through a fine sieve. Then stir in ½ cup of sour cream. Pour in a cup of sherry, a cup of cold water, and sweeten to taste with sugar. Chill thoroughly before using.

Or for the same number of servings, mash a quart of fresh, ripe blackberries with ¼ cup of honey, or puree them in the blender. Chill well and serve, perhaps further flavored with some good red wine to taste.

Elderberry Pie

You can make a straight elderberry (*Sambucus*) pie with the stewed fruit, sugar to taste, a melted tablespoon of butter for every cup of berries, and a little flour to absorb the excess juice and to provide a thicker syrup. But ripe elderberries and apples combine into an even more popular dessert.

Slice some tart apples into the lower ¾ of an uncooked shell, using the pastry recipe suggested for blackberry pie. Top with juicy, round, purplish black wild fruit. Sprinkle with a heaping cup of sugar mixed with 3 tablespoons flour and ⅛ teaspoon salt. Slice ½ stick of butter thinly over the top. Cover with a second crust.

Bake in a preheated hot 450° oven for 15 minutes. Then reduce the heat to a moderate 350° and bake for 35 to 40 minutes more, or until the crust is attractively brown. The taste, accented by the first perfumed breezes of evening, will be pungently pleasant.

Elderberry Fritters

For some really different fritters, gather some of the showy, flat-topped clusters of small white flowers of the common or American elderberry (*Sambucus canadensis*). Sprinkle these with brandy and confectioner's sugar. Then dip each bunch, with the tough stem snipped off, into a batter. Fry in deep hot fat until brown.

A fitting batter can be made by sifting together 2 cups of flour, a tablespoon of baking powder, and a teaspoon of salt. Beat 2 eggs. Add to them a tablespoon of molasses and a teaspoon of vanilla. Start with ⅔ cup of milk, adding more if necessary, so as to come up with a medium stiff batter. Quickly beat everything together until smooth. Use at once.

The hot elderberry fritters, cautiously handled so as not to mar the toothsome crust and briefly drained on absorbent paper, are a welcome adjunct to the main meal. Or you can dust them with sugar, and perhaps with cinnamon, and serve them with whipped cream for a light dessert.

Wild Strawberry Pie

When wild strawberries (*Fragaria*) are their juiciest and plumpest, it's pie time. Start by baking a deep pie shell with the pastry suggested for blackberry pie. Fill this, once it is well chilled, to within ½ inch of the top with the best of your berries, chilled for several hours in the refrigerator.

Then pack the pie shell firmly with strawberry ice cream that has been allowed to soften slightly. Preheat the oven to a hot 500° and have ready a meringue made with 4 egg whites. Allow the whites to come to room temperature after separating from the yolks, beat until just frothy, then add ½ teaspoon cream of tartar and continue beating until the egg whites are stiff but not dry. Take one tablespoon at a time, beat in a total of 8 tablespoons sugar, being certain that each addition of sugar is completely dissolved before the next is added. Swirl quickly over the ice cream, completely sealing the edge of the pastry. Pop into the oven for 3 minutes and serve at once.

Wild Strawberry Flapjacks

For something different from your regular flapjacks in strawberry country, slice 2 cups of fresh wild strawberries and leave them standing with 4 tablespoons sugar while you go about other chores. Then stir in 2 cups of sour cream, doing this lightly so as not to break up the berries. Spoon the results above and between each pair of steaming hot pancakes. This will really start the taste buds tingling.

Wild Strawberries Chantilly

Sometime when you have the desire for a taste sensation, start this delicacy by stemming 2 cups of your choicest fruit. Then whip 1½ cups of heavy cream with 2 tablespoons of confectioner's sugar and 2 tablespoons of brandy. Incidentally, Metaxa brandy will give this an elusive fragrance. Stir in the berries and set in the refrigerator for at least 2 hours.

Wild Strawberries and Champagne

"Most of our people went ashore upon the land of Cape Ann, which lay very near us, and gathered a store of fine strawberries," Governor John Winthrop of the Massachusetts Bay Colony wrote upon arriving off these rocky New England shores north of Boston in 1630.

Three centuries later, in almost the same spot, we first enjoyed the exquisite combination of wild strawberries and champagne. For four servings, carefully pick over 4 cups of the little crimson berries. Sprinkle them with 2 tablespoons sugar and put it in the refrigerator for several hours. Then immerse in a cup of well-chilled champagne and serve. The results will be fragile and evanescent.

Green Currant Pie

This is best when the currants (*Ribes*) are just starting to ripen. You'll need a quart. Mix them with 2 cups of sugar, a teaspoon cinnamon, ¼ teaspoon nutmeg, and either 3 table-spoons cornstarch or ⅓ cup flour.

The pastry suggested for blackberry pie is a good one for this double-crust pie, too. Bake in a hot 450° oven for 10 minutes. Then reduce the heat to a moderate 350° and bake 35 minutes more or until the crust is browned the way you like it. By then the room will be filled with the smell of spices and hot fruit.

Raspberry Pie

You'll need a baked pie shell to start with, a quart of chilled ripe raspberries (*Rubus*), a cup of confectioner's sugar, and ½ pint of heavy cream.

To make this pie shell, sift together a cup of sifted flour and ½ teaspoon salt. Cut in ¼ cup of shortening. Handling this lightly and quickly, add only enough water—about 3 tablespoons—to make a dough that will stay together when rolled. Roll out and place in a pie pan. Prick to prevent puffing. Bake in a hot 450° oven for 12 to 15 minutes or until done.

Line the baked and cooled shell with the soft raspberries. Sprinkle with confectioner's sugar. Add layer after layer until the fruit and the sugar are all used. Just before serving this pie, whip the cream and pour it in a fluffy white mound atop the crimson fruit.

Raspberry Sherbet

Heat the raspberries in a kettle with a cup of water for every gallon of fruit. Mash, stirring to prevent scorching. After 5 minutes of this, strain off the juice with the help perhaps of a jelly bag.

For every 2 cups of juice, add 1 cup sugar, 2 teaspoons cornstarch, 2 whole cloves, and a small piece of stick cinnamon. Bring just to a boil, simmer 1 minute, and remove spices. Then take off the heat and allow to cool.

Mix this cup of wild berry juice with a cup of orange juice and ¾ cup of grape juice. Freeze for sherbet what you don't serve on the spot with cracked ice. Both will take the edge off a heat-saturated day.

Wild Raspberry Butter

You'll find many uses for this gourmet butter, even to spreading it on crisp salted crackers for some unusual appetizers.

Just let a stick of butter soften at room temperature.

Then cream it with a cup of confectioner's sugar, using a spoon and adding the sweetening a bit at a time. Finally, stir and beat in ½ cup of crushed wild raspberries, flavored with ½ teaspoon vanilla. Keep covered in the refrigerator like regular butter.

Suntanned Wild Strawberry Jam

You sometimes come upon such luscious hordes of juice-bursting strawberries on a vacation that, although having no apparent facilities for so doing, you wish you could transport some of their bright red deliciousness back to the city canyons. Here's a gourmet pioneer method that has come delectably down through the years.

Clean your freshly picked ripe strawberries, put in a kettle with an equal volume of sugar, let stand ½ hour to begin releasing the juice, bring to a simmer, and allow to bubble slowly for 15 minutes. Then pour the colorful mixture in a thin layer on large platters, cover loosely with glass or with one of the handy plastics in dome form, and set in the direct sunlight. If the weather becomes stormy, move inside to a very, very slow oven, its door ajar.

Twice a day stir the berries thoroughly, being careful not to crush them and so spoil their exquisite appearance. After some 3 to 5 days of this, the fruit will be sufficiently preserved to keep. Stow in hot sterilized bottles and seal with paraffin for enjoyment when city streets have shut in about you once more.

Wild Cranberry Sauce

Sauce made with wild cranberries (*Vaccinium*), because they have more flavor and color than domestic varieties, affords an especially pungent supplement to game meat.

With the wild fruit, try simmering 2 cups sugar, 1½ cups water, and ½ cup sauterne for 5 minutes. Then lower the heat and mix a quart of cleaned wild cranberries with the syrup. Cook slowly without stirring, uncovered, for about 15 minutes or until the softened skins open. Skim off the froth. Cool, chill in the refrigerator, stir in a jigger of brandy, and serve to your delighted feasters who are gathered at the groaning board.

Wild Cranberry Pie

Made in double amounts, the pastry suggested for raspberry pie is fragile and flaky enough to go with the flavorful marvelousness of wild cranberries.

When this pastry is ready, mix 2 tablespoons flour, 1½ cups sugar, and ⅛ teaspoon salt. Add a cup of water, beat until smooth, and bring to a boil, stirring. Add 2 cups of wild cranberries and simmer until the berries are soft. Then remove from the heat and stir in a cup of seedless raisins and a teaspoon of vanilla.

Be preheating an oven to a hot 400°. Pour the filling into an uncooked lower pastry shell in a pie plate. Slice on thin chips of butter. Then cover with the upper pastry. Bake ½ hour or until the crust is well browned. Served warm with vanilla ice cream, this will really top off your meal.

Gooseberry Catsup

Important as Indian food, gooseberries (*Ribes*) were among the native American fruits quickly adopted by settlers and frontiersmen. A gourmet catsup made of them, excellent with game, was famous even back in Colonial days. Just simmer 5 pounds of stemmed and cleaned gooseberries, 4 pounds brown sugar, 2 cups cider vinegar, 1 tablespoon cinnamon, 2 teaspoons each of cloves and allspice, and ¼ teaspoon cayenne pepper for 2 hours. Then fill sterilized bottles, seal, and label.

Wild Blueberry Pie

For one 9-inch pie, pick over and wash a quart of blueberries (*Vaccinium*) (*Gaylussacia*). Put a cup of these into a saucepan along with 1¼ cups of sugar, 2 tablespoons butter, ⅛ teaspoon salt, and 2 tablespoons cornstarch mixed with ¼ cup of cold water. Cook over low heat until thick, stirring occasionally and crushing the fruit. Then remove from the stove, mix in a tablespoon lemon juice, pour over the remaining berries, and let stand until cold.

In the meantime, make your pastry. If you don't have a favorite recipe of your own, this may be started by sifting together 1¼ cups flour and ⅛ teaspoon salt. Cut in ¼ cup apiece of butter and of bear grease or commercial shortening, add 4 tablespoons cold water, and mix gently. Roll out thin. Line the pie dish or pan. Use the remaining pastry for strips to lay across the top of the pie.

Pour the filling into the uncooked pie shell, spread evenly, and lay on the latticework of upper crust. Bake in a moderate 375° oven about 50 minutes, or until the crust is golden brown.

Wild Blueberry Flapjacks

Wild blueberry flapjacks are something special the year around, bringing back as they do the familiar vision of the unspoiled earth, the murmur of insects, the distant cowbells, and the soft stirring of a light breeze. Make your regular batter and drop it, ⅓ cup at a time, on a hot griddle lightly greased with bacon rind. Do not let your griddle get so hot that it smokes.

If you're cooking for two and don't have a favorite flapjack recipe, sift together a cup of flour, a tablespoon of baking powder, a tablespoon of sugar, and ⅛ teaspoon of salt. Beat an egg with ⅔ cup of milk and 2 tablespoons melted butter. Add to the dry ingredients, mix quickly, and have everything ready to move without any waiting.

Sprinkle 2 tablespoons of blueberries over each saucer-sized flipper. When the hotcake begins showing small bubbles and its underside is golden, turn it and brown the other side. Have the butter dish loaded and enough syrup waiting to match the appetites.

Hot Wild Blueberry Sauce

This is particularly good when you're vacationing near wilderness burns where blueberries thrive, and there's a country store nearby that stocks vanilla ice cream. With the help of the freezer, of course, you can enjoy it in the city, too. Mix 2 cups of freshly washed blueberries, ½ cup sugar, ½ cup water, a teaspoon cinnamon, and ¼ teaspoon nutmeg. Boil 5 minutes, stirring well. Have the ice cream all ladled out, and spoon the hot fruit over each portion.

Steamed Wild Blueberry Pudding

Especially on a winter-shortened evening, sift together 2 cups sifted flour, a cup of sugar, a tablespoon baking powder, and a teaspoon salt. Cut or rub in ½ stick of butter until you have a coarse, crumbly mixture. Mix in 2 cups of blueberries.

Add a lightly beaten egg to 1¾ cups of milk. Stir into the dry ingredients only until everything is moistened. Immediately pour the batter into a buttered pan or mold, cover, and steam 2 hours.

This is good with a lemon sauce, made by mixing ½ cup sugar, a tablespoon cornstarch, and ¼ teaspoon salt. Gradually stir in a cup of boiling water. Boil 5 minutes. Then remove from the heat and add 3 tablespoons butter, a beaten egg yolk, ⅛ teaspoon cinnamon, and the juice of a good-sized lemon.

Wild Blueberry Muffins

For tender, perfect muffins and berries that stay almost as juicy as they were when freshly picked, mix the following ingredients lightly. Begin by gently beating an egg, then adding it to ½ cup of milk and mixing with ⅓ cup melted butter.

Sift together 1¾ cups sifted flour, a tablespoon baking powder, ½ cup sugar, and ¼ teaspoon salt. Then mix in a cup of plump blueberries as gently as possible. Pour in the combined milk, egg, and butter and stir quickly, only until everything is moistened.

Bake in a buttered muffin pan in a hot 400° oven for about 25 minutes, or until the tops are pleasingly brown. If you are not going to eat these immediately, tilt each muffin in its container to keep from steaming the crusts. Keep warm.

If any are left over, they are good cold. If you want to reheat them, though, just wrap loosely in aluminum foil and put in a hot 400° oven for about a dozen minutes. Either way, these will bring back the happy adventures of hot hillsides.

Baked Wild Blueberries

Mix a quart of blueberries with a cup of sugar, the juice of a lemon, and a tablespoon of grated lemon peel. Pour into a well-buttered baking dish.

Cream 5 tablespoons of butter and ½ cup of sugar. Beat an egg with ¼ teaspoon salt and add that. Mix well with ½ cup milk and a teaspoon of vanilla. Have everything ready to go. Then quickly stir in 1½ cups of sifted flour and 1½ teaspoons baking powder. Spread over the blueberries. Bake in a hot 400° oven about 25 minutes or until the top is golden.

Mulberry Pie

The ripe fruit of the red mulberry (*Morus*), resembling that of the blackberry in color as well as shape when it ripens to a dark purple, makes a long-remembered pie with a minimum of bother. The pastry recipe suggested for blueberry pie is an ideal one.

Just fill an uncooked pie shell with the fruit. Sprinkle with a cup of sugar mixed with ¼ cup flour, and the juice of a lemon. Add the second crust and bake in a moderate 375° oven about 50 minutes, or until the crust is your idea of a tempting brown. Served when a heady breeze is moving through the dining room, making the candles drip, this is really delicious.

Rum Cherry Foam

The rum cherries (*Prunus*) that grow plump and black over much of the East can be given a gourmet touch by first simmering, with a bit of water to prevent scorching, and straining enough of the fruit to give you ½ cup of concentrated juice.

In a heavy pan, combine the cherry juice and ½ cup light corn syrup and bring to a boil. Dissolve in this 2 cups sugar and a tablespoon of chipped lemon peel. Cook over moderate heat without stirring until a drop hardens when dropped into cold water (254° to 268° on your candy thermometer). Meanwhile, when the syrup is cooking, beat 3 egg whites in a large bowl until they are stiff but not dry.

When the syrup is ready, pour it slowly in a thin stream into the egg whites, beating constantly all the while. Continue beating until the mixture holds its shape, then drop onto waxed paper from a teaspoon. Arrange these on your prettiest dish, along with some candied wild mint leaves. This endeavor really makes an epicurean tableau of the venture of cooking wild fruit.

Juniper Berry Vinegar

A few juniper berries (*Juniperus*) tossed on the glowing coals of a barbecue fire just before you slap on those thick venison steaks will add a woodsy savor to the meat. These aromatic, cleanly astringent, berrylike fruits, used sparingly, will also do much for rabbit, duck, grouse, quail, and other game when used to flavor stuffings, marinades, and sauces. Dried, they keep indefinitely.

For a pleasantly perfumed vinegar to add to these latter two, drop a tablespoon of the small blue fruits into a quart of simmering cider vinegar, seal in a sterilized jar or bottle, label, and store in a cool dark sanctuary for at least a month before using.

Persimmon Pudding

Persimmons (*Diospyros*), sweetened by frost, were among the lifesaving edibles shown to the starving English settlers their first winter in Virginia by Indian neighbors who'd long mashed this agreeable fruit for cakes and puddings.

The wild persimmon, one of this country's most abundant and delicious tree fruits, still provides a luscious pudding when ripeness has mellowed away its puckery quality. Mix together a cup of sieved persimmon pulp, a cup of sugar, and 2 teaspoons of baking soda. Then stir in a cup of sifted flour, ½ cup sliced walnuts, ½ cup seedless raisins, ½ cup milk, 2 teaspoons melted butter, 1 teaspoon vanilla extract, ½ teaspoon cinnamon, ½ teaspoon ginger, and ⅛ teaspoon salt. Pour into a greased baking dish and bake in a preheated moderate 350° oven for an hour.

Find out which you prefer with this hot pudding, fresh thick cream or a hard sauce made by beating ½ cup butter with 1½ cups of gradually added confectioner's sugar.

Highbush Cranberry Jelly

Especially when I'm eating it along with sizzling moose steaks, I wouldn't swap the provocatively different jelly highbush cranberries (*Viburnum*) make for any other in the world. For a reddish orange, beautifully translucent jelly of singular flavor and ideal texture, gather the still firm fruit before the first really cold snap, while it is about half-ripe.

Bring each 2 cups of these berries to a simmer in three cups of water, mashing them as they dance. Keep bubbling for 5 minutes. Then strain out the skins and flattish seeds through a jelly bag. Stir ⅔ cup of sugar into each cup of juice and boil until jelly "sheets" from the spoon. Then tip into hot, sterilized glasses and seal immediately. A lot of people don't care for this somewhat sweetish-sour dainty at first, but with repeated samplings many of them come to agree that there's no other jelly quite as good.

Spiced Wild Berries

Spiced wild blueberries, gooseberries, and blackberries pleasantly supplement the heavier game meats such as moose and bear and the fatter fish such as whitefish, catfish, and salmon. The berries are best when slightly on the green side.

For each pound of fruit, add ½ cup of cider vinegar and a cup of preferably brown sugar. Boil the vinegar and sugar together until the latter is completely dissolved. Then add the fruit.

For the above proportions, tie a teaspoon of cinnamon, ¼ teaspoon cloves, ¼ teaspoon nutmeg, and ⅛ teaspoon allspice in a cloth, leaving the string long enough so you can retrieve the spice bag after it has been immersed in the simmering berries for ½ hour.

Then, if you're putting up some, pour the hot fruit into sterilized jars and seal immediately. See if this doesn't bring back the memory of some particularly pleasurable berry-gathering afternoon when a light breeze has sprung up, heavy with the smell of water.

Wild Fruit Sauce

A lot of people just boil their fruit with a little water and with sugar to taste and let it go at that, but the pick of the wild fruits are worth a bit more effort. For a notable sauce, try bringing 2 cups of the fruit juices, 1½ cups sugar, and 2 tablespoons cornstarch to a simmer, all the time stirring.

Then remove from the heat and mix in ½ stick of butter and a tablespoon of lemon juice. When you are ready, put in 2 cups of crushed fruit, return to the stove, and stir until thick.

Incidentally, a particularly effective sauce is made by combining wild strawberries and raspberries in equal amounts. Such wild fruit sauces are nothing less than superb both hot and when chilled.

Vacation Mousse

Two cups of strawberries, raspberries, salmonberries, blackberries, or similar wild fruit, plus an equal volume of whipped cream, will give you four servings of unforgettable wild berry mousse. You may care to stir in a little sugar to taste.

If you are vacationing away from your normal base of supplies, you may be restricted to making your whipped cream from ordinary evaporated milk. However, this can be simplicity itself if you first make sure that milk and utensils are icy cold, perhaps from being submerged in a mountain stream.

So chilled, most evaporated milk rapidly whips to about triple volume. Several teaspoons of lemon juice, canned or fresh, can be used to heighten the stiffness once the milk is properly whipped. You also can employ for this purpose an envelope of unflavored gelatin, softened in ¼ cup of cold water in a custard cup, then set in a pan of hot water and stirred until dissolved.

Wild Berry Shortcake

To match 6 cups of berries, freshly picked or thawed and left standing drenched with a cup of sugar, sift together for the biscuit dough 2 cups sifted flour, a tablespoon baking powder, ½ teaspoon salt, and ⅛ teaspoon nutmeg. Cut in a stick of butter until everything is the consistency of coarse corn meal.

Then beat an egg, add ¾ cup light cream, and mix lightly with the flour mixture. Shape half the dough gently into a buttered 8-inch pan. Brush the top with melted butter. Pat the remaining half atop that. Bake in a preheated hot 450° oven about 20 minutes or until done.

Split the hot shortcake. Spread the bottom half liberally with butter that has been allowed to soften to room temperature. Then spoon on half the berries. Replace the steaming top and sluice that down with the remaining fruit.

Cover either with whipped cream or, for a luxurious old-fashioned touch, with sour cream sweetened to taste.

Strawberries, blueberries, raspberries, blackberries, and similar wild fruits make this hot shortcake as happy a gustatory experience as can come to mortal man.

Hot Berry Roll

You also can cook your shortcake in a single operation, creating a hot berry roll that is delicious "as is," or with vanilla ice cream, whipped cream, or a judicious dab of sour cream.

Make the same biscuit dough as for berry shortcake, kneading it briefly on a floured board or piece of plastic, but this time rolling it thinner. Dot it with bits of butter. Then spread on, as evenly as possible, 2 cups of blackberries, blueberries, or saskatoons that have been left standing drenched with ½ cup of sugar.

Roll up like a jelly roll, carefully transfer to a greased metal sheet or shallow pan, and bake in a moderate 350° oven about 40 minutes, or until satisfyingly golden—just enough time to give the fruit blanketed within an added savor.

This is good when sliced and served cold. But you owe it to yourself to try at least part of it hot, when, in addition to its deliciousness, it provides an olfactory adventure of the highest order.

Index of Recipes

Abalone, fried, 154
  steaks 153
Amaranth soufflé 190
Angelica, soup 164
Arctic grayling omelet 133

Bass, baked 128
  smallmouth 128
Bear, chops 39
  cracklings 39
  roast 37
  stew 38
Beaverburgers 86
Beaver, roast 84
  beaver tail soup 85
Berries, 198-219 *(see wild berries)*
  Hot berry roll 219
Blackberry, pie 200
  soup 201
Blue gills 129
Blueberries (wild), baked 212
  flapjacks 210
  muffins 212
  pie 209
  pudding 211
  sauce 211
Brunswick stew 97
Buffalo hump 41
Bullhead chowder 130

Caribou 41
Cattail hotcakes 181

Chickweed omelet 192
Clams, 139-144
  Angels on horseback 144
  baked 141
  cakes 143
  chowder 140
  Clam pie 142
  fried 143
  grilled 143
  quick 139
  steamed 140
Cocktail sandwiches 173
Coot, roast 55
Cougar 109
Crab, cakes 149
  crab meat salad 148
  Crab Newburg 148
  baked 147
Cranberries (wild), pie 208
  sauce 208
Crayfish, bisque 149
  patties 150
Crow, breasts 75
  with rice 76
Currant pie 205

Dandelion greens, creamed, 180
  soup 180
Dove, potted 71
  roast 72
  sautéed 71
  stewed 70
Duck (wild), braised 53

Duck (wild), breast, sautéed 55
    broiled 54
    roast 50, 51, 52

Eel, broiled 132
Elderberry, fritters 202
    pie 201

Fiddleheads, 195
    salad 196
Fireweed and eggs 171
Fish balls 132
Fisherman's respite 133
Fish loaf 133
Frog legs, broiled 104
    grilled 103
    sautéed 102

Game, "boiled" 26
Gameburgers 30
Goose (wild), pâté 70
    roast 68
Gooseberry catsup 209
Grilse, planked 124
Groundnut omelet 194
Grouse, broiled 49
    creamed 50
    roast 48
    spitted 47

Ham and mustard green soup
    183
Hare, "jugged" 89
Hasenpfeffer 92
Hash, big game 36
Heart, big game 33
Highbush cranberry jelly 215

Horseradish, dip 188
Horseradish, sauce 188
    soup 187

Jerusalem artichoke, salad 191
    sautéed 190
    soup 191
Juniper berry vinegar 214

Kabobs, small game 110
Kidneys, broiled 33
    flambé 35
    sautéed 34

Lamb's lettuce salad 185
Lamb's-quarters salad 179
Ling liver 134
Liver, big game 31
Liver and bacon 32

Marrow 31
Miner's lettuce au gratin 185
Mint (wild), candied 189
    sauce 189
Moose nose 40
Mountain sheep 43
Mountain sorrel, soufflé 162
    soup 162
    with eggs 161
Mulberry pie 213
Mulligan 28
Muskrat, roast 107
Muskrat stew 108
Mussels, bisque 151
    fried 150
    soup 152
    simmered 152

Mustard, soup 179, 177
Mustard, molds 178
　with scrambled eggs 177

Nettle balls 172

Onions (wild), and bear 176
　and toast 175
　sauce 173
　soup 174
Opossum, and sassafras 99
　baked 99
　broiled 99
　roast 98
Oysters, baked 147
　Oysters Beverly 145
　broiled 144
　minced 146
　scalloped 146

Partridge, and rice 59
　breast of 58
　in mustard leaves 57
　northern 56
　roast 57
　sandwiches 59
Pasties, trading post 60
Persimmon pudding 215
Pheasant, braised 65
　broiled 64
　hash 67
　in cream 65
　roast 64
　with water cress 66
Pickerel, baked 129
Pigeon, potted 71
　roast 72

Pigeon, sautéed 71
　stewed 70
Plantain, roast 183
　with vinegar sauce 182
Porcupine, liver 105
　stew 104
Purslane salad 183

Quail, 61
　broiled 63
　camp-style 62
　in sour cream 63
　roast 62

Rabbit, and noodles 91
　and split peas 89
　baked 87
　fried 87
　marinated 94
　oven 88
　roast 93
　stew 90
　with sherry 91
Raccoon, roast 106
Ragout, small-game 110
Raspberry (wild), butter 206
　pie 205
　sherbet 206
Rum cherry foam 213

Salmon, Atlantic poached 124
　grilse, planked 124
　loaf 127
　poached 126
　sautéed 125
Scallops, broiled 155
　sautéed 155
Scotch lovage, braised 163

Sea moss blancmange 195
Shepherd's-purse, wilted 182
Snipe, broiled 73
  roast 73
Squirrel, broiled 96
  Brunswick stew 97
  marinated 94
  roast 97
  sautéed 95
Strawberries (wild), and champagne 204
  Chantilly 204
  flapjacks 204
  jam 207
  pie 203
Sunflower seed soup 193
Sweet flag, candied 193

Tongue, big game 35
Trout, brook, baked 117
  brook, broiled 121
  brook, spitted 120
  fried 115
  grilled 116
  lake, baked 118
  lake, with mint 121
  lamé 118
  meunière 120
  oven-fried 116
  poached 123
  rainbow, in white wine 119
  sautéed 122
  with almonds 123
Turkey (wild), ovenless 78
  roast 77
Turtle, soup 156
  stew 155
  Turtle Stroganoff 157

Vacation mousse 217
Venison, cutlets 19, 20
  dumplings 27
  meat loaf 27
  pot roast 23
  ribs 24, 25
  roast 20
  steaks and onions 18
  steak, broiled 15
  steak, grilled 14
  steak, pan-broiled 15
  steaks with pepper 17
  steaks with wine 16
  tenderloin 16

Water cress, fried 170
  salad 168
  sandwiches 167
  with eggs 169
  hot weather salad, 169
Wild berries, spiced 216
Wild berry shortcake 218
Wild fruit sauce 217
Wild giblet soup 76
Wild leeks and eggs 176
Wild lettuce, salad 184
  soup 186
Wild rice, 164
  wild rice mold 165
  with livers 166
Winter cress soup 170
Woodchuck, braised 100
  soup 101, 102
  stew 100
Woodcock
  fried 75
  with cream 74